How to be BETTER at NETWORKING

In Person and Online

Mike Grocott

Copyright © 2021 Mike Grocott

All rights reserved.

No portion of this book may be reproduced, stored in a retrieval system or transmitted in any form or means (including electronic, mechanical, photocopy, recording, scanning or other) without prior permission from the copyright holder, except for brief quotations in critical reviews or articles.

ISBN: 9798740691862

Cover design by Dave Brogden.

Acknowledgements

To Tony, from whom I learnt so much in my early days.

To Andy, for his ideas that inspired my own.

To Dom, whose keen eye, insight and observations made this a better book.

To Charlie, for her encouragement and feedback and her greatly valued experience, guidance and help with the Social Media aspects of this book.

And to Daryl, my third ever connection, the biggest positive influence on my network (and therefore my business), without whose generosity of time, direction and connections the last decade or so would have been very different.

Contents

About this Book 1
Part 1 7
    The Foundations of Networking 9
    Networking: A Definition 11
    Don't Sell, Build! 13
    Joining the Dots 17
    The Confidence Formula 21
Part 2 23
    How to Prepare for Networking Events 25
    The RAIL Framework 27
    The ICE Framework 53
Part 3 57
    How to be Confident at Networking Events 59
    The Confidence Cycle 61
    The PROWESS Framework 63
    The SHINE Framework 77
    Thought for Food 81
    The HELPful Introduction 83
    Think HRH 85
Part 4 89
    Networking on Social Media 91
    The A to D of Social Media Involvement 93
    Define and Find your Audience 97
    Have Clear Aims 101
    Be Effective, not Busy 105
    Be Interesting and Sociable 111
Further Information 119
    The *"Interact better. Achieve more."* Series 121
    About the Author 123

About this Book

I used to hate networking.

In fact, I used to hate networking a lot!

It was 2009 and I had just returned to my native Staffordshire to set up my own business. I had no clients. I had no prospective clients. At least I did have a network of business contacts, all two of them.

So I needed to get out there and make new contacts or my business would fail. I needed to go networking and I hated it – a lot!

Cleaning, ironing and even gardening all seemed so much more appealing than going networking and I *really* don't like cleaning, ironing or gardening.

So I went networking. I had to.

I can clearly remember my first networking event: the venue, the person I was introduced to first, the four people who sat around the table when we had lunch. I was on public show and I didn't know what to do, I didn't know what to say. It was a very uncomfortable experience and those memories are etched indelibly into my mind in the same way as breaking a leg would be.

But I persevered. I had to.

Over the next few months and years, however, I started to meet some very welcoming people, people who were generous with their time, their contacts and their knowledge. I still didn't really know what I was doing but I was getting better at networking. My network was growing, my business was growing, I was achieving some success. I was even starting to feel more confident when I was networking.

I was starting to dislike networking less.

So I persevered. I had to. But now I also wanted to.

There was still a lot to learn (and there still is, by the way) but I was a better networker, I was more confident and I was achieving more through my networking activities.

Fast forward to today and my network has hundreds of contacts in it, my business is flourishing and I actually now like networking – a lot!

So it's fair to say that since 2009 I have learned many things about networking. Some of that has come from those generous people I mentioned earlier without whom my network, and therefore my business, wouldn't be what it is today.

Some of it, of course, has come from the mistakes I have made along the way and I shudder to think of how much time and money I have wasted over the years!

At some point along my own learning journey, I started to help other people to be better at networking. Although I might not remember exactly when that was (I think it was about 2013), I do remember why I started doing it. It was to spare them the pain that I went through myself. I had been fortunate to have been given the insight and experience of some generous people that had made a hugely positive influence on me and my business. Now it was my turn to be the one making a difference for others.

So I now train and coach other people to be better, more confident networkers. By doing so I help them to develop the knowledge and skills that will help them to get more out of their networking activities.

I also design and facilitate a variety of networking events for organisations, delivered both in person and online. Through these events, my goal is to help people to make those connections in the most effective, pain-free ways that I can (and for them to have some fun whilst they are doing it too!).

Over the years, through my training, coaching and facilitation, I have therefore created, refined and used a number of guides, ideas and frameworks to help people to be better at networking. (I'll collectively refer to them as "frameworks" from now on for simplicity.) Their goal is to be simple enough to be remembered, easy enough to be put into practice and robust enough to actually be of some use in the first place!

In this book you will therefore find that collection of frameworks. Simply put, what these frameworks will provide you with is the knowledge and skills on *how* to be a better networker.

If you know how to be a better networker then when you put that new knowledge and skills into practice you will *be* a better networker. If you are better when you network, then your networking will be more effective and more successful. That will give you more confidence for your next networking activities which will in turn make you an even better networker.

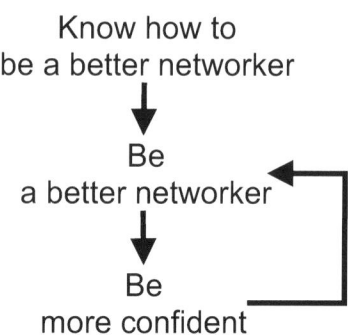

So there is a cyclical aspect to this but there is a clear place to start: know *how* to be a better networker.

And this book will show you *how* to be a better networker so you can *be* a better networker and therefore more confident when networking.

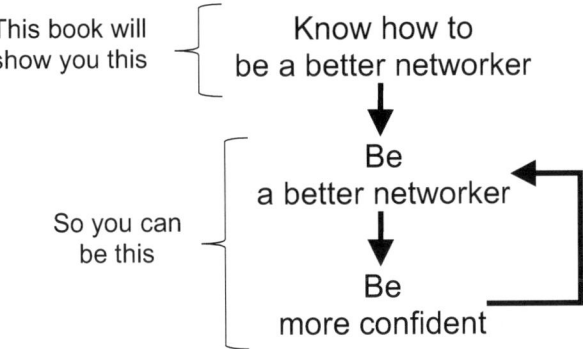

And by being a better, more confident networker it will help you to achieve what you want, whatever that may be.

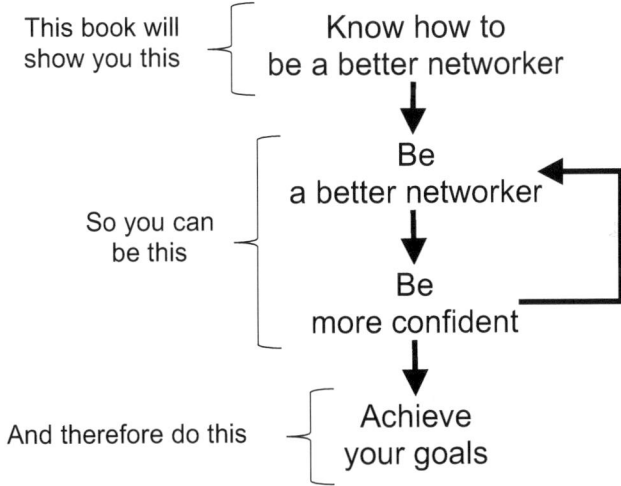

To get the most out of this book I would suggest that you first read this book from front to back as that represents the logical and chronological approach that you would take to going networking.

Once you've done that you can dip in and out of the book as required as the frameworks are essentially standalone in nature focusing on particular aspects of networking. That being said, the different frameworks are interrelated and do cross-reference each other on occasion.

Due to the circular nature of the cross-references, sometimes I'll mention something in passing that I will cover later in detail in the book. For clarity, I'll highlight those occurrences with an arrow and highlight to which future section the reference applies.

There are also some other callouts that are highlighted in this book:

 *This book can also be used as a workbook, to help you as you actually go through the process of preparing to network. I've created a number of resources that are available from the Resources section of my website: www.intercog.co.uk.*

 *To supplement the material in this book, I have also created some video content. (it's sometimes easier to show you than tell you) These video resources are also available from the Resources section of my website: www.intercog.co.uk.*

 *People that know me well would tell you that I like a good tangent and so you'll find a few of these tangents as you go through the book. They are not core to the book but will add some personal asides, notes and references that are relevant at that point.*

Online Considerations

A huge amount of networking activity takes place face-to-face where you are actually there in person. Examples of these occasions are regular networking groups, networking events, conferences, exhibitions, awards ceremonies etc.

Over recent times, some of these more traditionally in-person networking occasions have moved online as technology has allowed this to happen and circumstances have dictated that this is how it needed to be done.

For the purposes of categorisation, I'll therefore refer to these more traditional activities like those above as "events", for both the in-person and online versions.

There is also the world of Social Media where a lot of networking activities happen. Applications such as LinkedIn, Facebook and Twitter all provide an infrastructure through which networking can be done. I'll group these together under the category of "Social Media" for the purposes of this book.

Regardless of the activity being performed, however, there are also some fundamental aspects that need to be considered regarding networking, considerations that apply to both events and Social Media, to both in-person and online activities.

Pictorially, they fit together like this:

In Person	Online
Events	Social Media
Foundations of Networking	

Part 1 of this book will therefore look at the foundations that apply to all networking activities.

For events, there are things that need to be considered before the event and things that need to be considered during the event and so each aspect has its own section within the book:

- Part 2: How to Prepare for Networking Events
- Part 3: How to be Confident at Networking Events

Within each of these sections I will cover both the in-person and online aspects of events.

The final section of this book will then address networking using Social Media. In this section I'll look not only at those principles that can be taken from the events-side of networking and applied to Social Media but also those that are new to this environment, all with the goal of helping you to make your Social Media networking more effective.

Note: I won't be going into technical details here for each of the Social Media platforms. That is not the purpose of this book.

As a final comment about this book, I have structured it to allow me to focus on events and Social Media separately. They are, however, not mutually exclusive. In fact, to be better at networking as a whole, I would suggest that you need to be attending meetings *and* using Social Media. What percentage of your time is spent doing which is, of course, up to you!

So let's start by looking at the foundations of networking…

Part 1

The Foundations of Networking

There are some fundamental principles that relate to networking and apply regardless of how it is that you are doing your networking. These principles are examined in turn in this part of the book.

The first of these is to simply define what networking is in its simplest form.

Next, it's about having a very clear idea of what networking is really all about and, equally as importantly, what it is not. In many ways it's a mindset thing and as with all mindsets, having the right one helps and the wrong one hinders!

The third principle is that networking is not an overnight thing. It takes time and effort. You can't just snap your fingers and a network appears.

The child in me is now imagining Mr Benn in the costume shop and a network appearing, as if by magic!

If only that were the case...

Earlier in the book I was talking about how confidence comes from being better at networking and that, in turn, being more confident then leads to being a better networker. It is possible to look more closely at where confidence comes from and therefore how to be more confident.

So the greater the confidence, the more effective the networking and this is the fourth fundamental principle that applies to networking (and many other things of course!).

Networking: A Definition

For defining what networking is in its simplest form.

I have a question for you:

>What is networking?

It's a question I ask of people when I'm doing training and working with people as a coach. As you can imagine, I get quite a variety of answers!

I'm curious, therefore, what your answer to that question would be. How would you define what networking is? How would you answer that question?

Having asked you for your answer, it seems only fair that I should now offer my own answer to that question. In essence, I define networking to be:

>interacting with other people

Yes, I believe it's as simple as that!

Any time that you are interacting with other people you are networking. So that could mean any of these occasions:

- a breakfast meeting for a group dedicated to networking
- a networking event
- a conference
- a trade show
- posting on Social Media
- chatting to people *within* your business (you can network with people you work with too)
- playing golf
- jogging with your running club

If you stop and think for a moment about all of the ways and occasions that you interact with other people then that's a very long list! Every entry on that list is an opportunity for networking.

Using that premise as the basis for what networking is, therefore, means that you can apply the knowledge and skills presented in this book for any of those occasions. Clearly, there will be different amounts of application on different occasions but the principle still holds.

However, there is one more thing that needs to be considered here: how to make your networking *effective*, i.e. how to get the most out of your activities.

To that end, a small tweak to the definition is required:

effective networking is *purposefully* interacting with others

The addition of *purposefully* implies:

- having clear goals for what you want to achieve
- putting realistic timeframes on when those goals will be achieved
- preparing properly
- having a plan for what you are going to do
- developing the skills needed to execute that plan successfully
- executing the plan with confidence

Having this purposeful approach, therefore, works towards combatting some of the things that prevent people from networking effectively, e.g.:

- fear
- lack of confidence
- not knowing who to talk to
- not knowing what to say
- not knowing what to do
- having a misguided belief that results will come quickly

So this book will show you how to purposefully interact with other people, with greater confidence, because that's all effective networking really is.

Don't Sell, Build!

For clarifying what the best way to approach networking is (and isn't).

Let's start at the beginning.

Why do *you* go networking?

Here's a space for you to put your answers:

And from your experiences of meeting other people, why do you think *they* go networking? (in addition to what you have above)

And here's another space for those answers:

I would speculate that your answers above might include some of the following:
- to meet people
- to make new connections
- to arrange follow-on meetings
- to catch up with people you already know
- to be seen
- to promote your business
- to be liked
- to talk about successes
- to gather information (on competitors, the market, best practices etc.)
- to partake in the free food and drink
- to ~~sell to other people~~
- to **build relationships**

However, you'll notice that two entries on the list are different in style from the others:
- I've crossed out "sell to other people" because networking is not about selling
- I've emboldened "build relationships" because that's what networking is really all about

Some people think that the best approach to take when networking is to try and sell you something. They are the people that unsolicitedly thrust their business card at you within the first few seconds of meeting you, they go on and on about their products and services and wax lyrical about why if you bought them your world would be a better place.

I suspect you might have met them! And if you have, how have you reacted?

Exactly!

Whereas if you focus on building relationships, on getting to know others and helping them to get to know you, then your networking will be much more effective. The more you understand them, the more you'll appreciate:
- what they do
- why they do it
- how they do it
- and what they need to help them to do it

The more they understand you, the more they'll appreciate those things for you too. And if you build those relationships, then business will come, when it is ready to come.

To misquote Kevin Costner from the film "Field of Dreams":

If you build the relationships, business will come!

People ultimately buy from people and then only from people they know, like and trust. That means that the focus needs to be on the building of the relationships, not the act of selling.

Not that I'm saying, of course, that sales and revenue are not important. They clearly are! They are, however, the result of the relationships that you build whilst networking and not what you need to be focussing on whilst you are networking.

So don't sell, build!

Joining the Dots

For painting the big picture that networking takes patience, practice and purpose.

I grew up in Staffordshire, went to university in Birmingham and, after graduating, spent nearly twenty years working "down south". I then came back to my native Staffordshire and set up my own business with the goal of only working in and around the local area.

At that point in time, the number of local contacts I had in my business network was two, two people who I knew from school who had stayed to work in the local area and, it has to be said, done very well for themselves!

Pictorially, it looked like this:

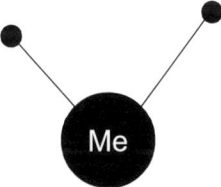

One of my two contacts suggested that I should meet with Daryl Williams, the coordinator of Finest which is the Professional Services networking organisation within Staffordshire Chambers of Commerce.

So I met with Daryl and she suggested that I should meet with a few more people who were also Finest members. My network had evolved:

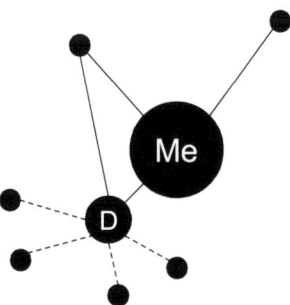

I was now connected to Daryl (bottom left) and you'll notice the line between my original contact (top left) and Daryl as they already knew each other. There are four more contacts in my network but the lines to those are dotted as I had not met them at that point.

Over time, as I met more people, my network grew to look a bit more like this:

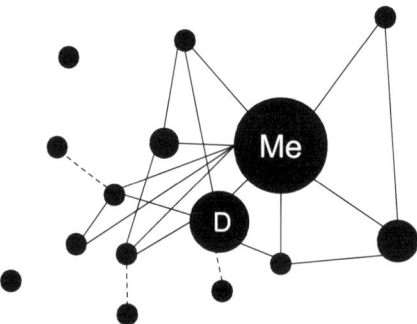

You'll notice that three of the connections from Daryl now link directly to me as I had now met them. You'll also noticed that there's still a dotted line from Daryl to one of her original suggestions. It's not always possible to meet everyone straight away!

There are some more dotted lines representing people that I wanted to be introduced to by people I already knew. You'll also notice some dots which have no connected lines. These are people that I knew I wanted to connect with but, at that moment in time, didn't know anyone who knew them.

The final observation that I would make is that some of the dots, e.g. Daryl's, are now also bigger. That's because by then I had developed a better, stronger relationship with those people. The effectiveness of a network isn't just about the number of people in it, i.e. the number of dots, it's also very much about the strength of the relationships with those people, i.e. the size of the dots. Having more, bigger dots is the goal.

Over time my network grew and there is no way that it would now be able to fit on a single page of this book! (If I were to draw a picture of it, though, it would have a lot of dots in it, of all sorts of sizes)

And that's a key concept – it takes time to develop your network. It's not an overnight thing. Sometimes it takes a while just to make that initial contact, let alone develop the relationship with that contact, let alone possibly to then do business with them.

So it takes **patience**.

What it also takes is **practice**.

The more you network, the better you will get (especially if you know a good book on how to do that!). The other thing about practice is that you have to do it. To get better you have to go out and network. That's the thing with things that require practice: how much you get out is directly proportional to how much you put in.

And the final thing that it takes is **purpose**.

It's very easy to spend a lot of time networking and not see any return on the investment of that time.

It's very easy to make a lot of contacts who are not the right sort of contacts for you.

It's very easy to have many, many contacts in your network without having a decent business relationship with any of them.

There has to be a purpose to your networking activities or you won't achieve what you want to. As I said earlier:

> *effective* networking is *purposefully* interacting with others

And you have to start with that purpose (and then practise and have patience).

T

Luck also plays its part on occasion!

One of my best clients came about purely because I happened to be randomly seated next to them at an awards ceremony. Had I been placed on a different table I might never have met them.

That being said, I had chosen to go to that event with the intention of meeting new people (purpose) and it took time and effort (and chocolate Hobnob biscuits incidentally) to develop that ultimately mutually beneficial relationship (practice and patience).

The Confidence Formula

For defining and understanding the building blocks of confidence.

The Confidence Formula is very simple:

C = A + P + S

That's the easy to remember mnemonic!

(I'll also refer to it in this book as the **CAPS** Framework.)

Expanding it into a slightly fuller format:

Confidence = **A**udience-focus + **P**reparation + **S**kills

In other words, how confident you are is the sum total of how much you consider your audience, how much preparation you do and how skilled you are at networking.

NOTE: In a networking context, the term "audience" here relates to the other people with whom you are interacting.

The more you do with regard to each of these three aspects, the more confident you will be.

The less you do, the less confident you'll be.

And if you ignore one aspect (or two), you won't be as confident as you could be.

It's a bit like a three-legged stool at a breakfast-bar in a kitchen:

- the legs need to be long enough for it to be useful as a stool when you sit next to the bar so you can eat your breakfast
- if the legs are not long enough, although you might be able to sit on your stool (it might be uncomfortable), you certainly wouldn't be able to reach your breakfast
- and if one leg or two legs are a lot shorter than the others, you won't be able to actually sit on it at all

The goal is to have a stool (C) with long-enough legs of similar lengths (APS).

The frameworks in this book will therefore look at these three different aspects of the Confidence Formula and show you how to have a better focus on your audience, be better prepared and have better all-round networking skills.

They are all about creating a taller more usable stool, as it were.

> *Before I move on to those frameworks, I have a quick tangent for you on over-confidence.*
>
> *Over-confidence comes from a false belief or self-perception by someone that their audience-focus, preparation and/or skills are at a higher level than they actually are in reality. Over-confidence can also come from a lack of being bothered. Whatever the cause, people who are over-confident are less likely to be effective when they network and more likely not to create as good an impression as they could.*
>
> *It is essential, therefore, to have an accurate, reflective and honest understanding of where you really are with regard to your audience-focus, preparation and skills.*
>
> *After all, trying to sit on a stool that's not as big as you thought it was, never ends well...*

Part 2

How to Prepare for Networking Events

"Fail to prepare and prepare to fail."

It's an old adage that applies to many, many things including going networking.

When thinking about how to be an effective networker, many people focus on the event itself and pay little attention to what they need to do before they get to the event.

Whilst there are indeed many things to consider in regard to how to be effective at the event itself (which I will cover in Part 3), there are an equal number of things that need to be considered before the event happens. In many ways, failing to do this preparation correctly, or at all, has an even bigger impact on networking effectiveness than what you might (or might not) do at the event.

This part of the book therefore looks at what needs to be done in preparation of your going networking so that when you get there you can be as ready as possible and therefore as effective as possible.

So I've got two frameworks for you here, frameworks that are tried, tested and proven to work, frameworks that together will help you to be as ready as you can be to go networking.

The RAIL Framework

For helping you to keep your networking activities on track.

The **RAIL** Framework is a four-part acronymic guide.

It represents a step-by-step, sequential approach to take when preparing to go networking. It will help you work out what you want to get from your networking and how you can go about achieving that.

Let's examine each letter in turn.

RAIL

It's essential to start at the beginning:

> What are your **Reasons** for going networking?

In other words, why are you spending all of this time (and money) going networking? What are your goals for attending?

One of the main reasons that people ask me to help them with their networking is because they feel that they are not getting much out of their time spent networking.

When I then ask them, "So what are you looking to get out of your networking, why are you going?" they often struggle to give me a definitive, quantitative answer. It's often something like: "more business", "better contacts", "a bigger network".

It's hardly surprising that their efforts are not very effective if they don't have a clear idea of why they are going networking in the first place...

So, linking back to what I was saying in the **Don't Sell, Build** Framework, the fundamental reason for networking is to build relationships. However, to do that there are a number of more specific reasons which might be along the lines of:

- to meet people
- to make new connections
- to arrange follow-on meetings
- to catch up with people you already know
- to promote your business
- to talk about successes
- to gather information (on competitors, the market, best practices etc.)

Your reasons will also vary from event to event and it's quite correct that they should. So you need to think about why you are networking and what it is that you are aiming to achieve and you need to do this for each and every event that you go to.

It's also important to evaluate the effectiveness of your networking and to do that you'll need something to measure, some quantifiable/SMART goals, and you'll need them for each event that you attend.

Having goals set at an individual event level will also allow you to evaluate the different networking events that you attend. This in turn will allow you to determine the return on investment that those events are providing and therefore which are (or are not) worth continuing to attend in the future.

The overall effectiveness of your networking will therefore be the sum total of the effectiveness of each individual event and many businesses set goals at this higher, longer-term level as well. These are the larger goals towards which the smaller goals are stepping-stones.

Many businesses will assign revenue targets for networking activities and this is perfectly understandable. It's important to remember, though, that business (i.e. revenue) comes from the relationships that are developed whilst networking and that it's therefore about building, not selling.

So you need to think about your goals *before* you attend the event. However, you can't really do that properly without also thinking about who else might be there, which is something I'll come back to in a moment.

The final reason that it's a good idea to think about your reasons for going networking is that in doing so it allows you to work out which events to attend and, conversely, which to not attend. There are lots of factors to consider here including:

- the event's location
- the time of day
- who might be there (which links to the next section)
- who you know who might be there
- how productive the event has been in the past

Having a clear idea of your reasons for networking will help you to evaluate which events to attend and which not, so you can increase the effectiveness of your time spent networking and reduce "wasted" time.

I've met many people who seem to go to every event that they can, simply because they can. Doing something simply because you can is not always a good reason for doing something...

rAIL

The next step is to think about your **Audience**, i.e. the other people at the event. There are a number of considerations here:

- Who is your target audience?
- What are your *real* goals for that audience?
- What is your plan for approaching your target audience?
- What do you know about your target audience?
- What if your target audience isn't available?
- Do you actually need to take a targeted approach?
- Is it OK to just talk to people you know?

Who is your target audience?

To work out who your target audience is, you need to think about the attendees that might be at the event. It is therefore important to spend some time prior to an event thinking about who will be there.

You might know this in advance if the organiser has sent out a delegate list prior to the event. If they haven't, you can ask them for one. They might not provide you with one but if they do it's a bonus! If they don't, then you lose nothing by asking.

If you haven't got a delegate list then you can speculate and hypothesise on who might be there.

Knowing or speculating on who will be there prior to the event will help with determining who your target audience is and in setting your goals for the event.

Of course, it might be the case that when you arrive at the event you are given a delegate list. Make the most of that information that you now have before you do anything else.

Many people take the delegate list, say thanks and then wander into the room, their biggest concern being what to do with the awkward piece of paper that they now need to carry. The organisers have given it to you for a reason – to help you to make the most of their event. So take a moment to use it. Find a quiet area and take a look at it. Compare it to your goals and, if needed, adjust those goals as required based on your new information.

It might also be the case that you have no delegate list at all, in advance or at the event. One possible workaround for this is to get to the event early and take a discreet look at the nicely laid out name badges on the reception desk as you arrive, assuming they have them of course...

So for your networking to be effective you need to take a targeted approach with respect to with whom you want to talk. Thinking about how you could segment the attendees can help you to do this. You could segment on:

- people you know versus people you don't know
- named individuals, e.g. John Smith from ABC Industries
- specific companies
- industries/business sectors
- roles within a business
- levels within a business
- size of business (employers, turnover etc)
- etc

These segments could be combined, e.g.:

- the HR Director at XYZ Accountants
- directors of IT companies
- senior managers in companies larger than 150 people in the pharmaceuticals sector
- etc

Once you have worked out your targets, then it's important to bring a SMART element to them. So, for example, how many directors of IT companies would it be *realistic* to talk to given the length of the event?

If you work that out, then you will be able to measure afterwards how many you did indeed talk to and gauge the effectiveness of that event. Also, by quantifying your objectives you will, over time, be able to get a better idea of what is realistic and this will help with avoiding over ambitious or optimistic objectives in the future.

Of course, if your target audience doesn't turn up then there's nothing you could do about that and so take that into consideration when you are judging effectiveness.

What are your *real* goals for that audience?

Having a conversation with your target audience is clearly a goal for a networking event. But what would you *really* like to get out of the event with regard to that audience? What would be a good "next step" in the journey of building a better relationship with that person?

For a new, or fairly new connection, it's probably a follow-on meeting, another opportunity to talk to them but this time without everyone else there so you can have them to yourselves, so to speak. In other words, a better "quality" of encounter.

I would proffer that a follow-on meeting is what the *real* goal is for you. So if during your conversation with them you decide that you do want to continue to build that relationship, make sure that you ask them for a follow-on meeting.

So be polite. Be bold. Be proactive.

Ask them there and then at the event (politely of course) if they would like to meet up and when would be good for them to do that.

Don't offer to contact them after the event to set up the follow-on meeting. Waiting until after the event to arrange the meeting is never as effective as doing it at the event itself. When you are talking to them at the event their focus and attention is on you and you have a direct conduit to them for pretty much instant decisions. If you leave it until after the event you lose all of those advantages and you are also reliant on them remembering who *you* are, as opposed to all of the other people they met at the event as well.

So be politely bold and take action at the event itself.

Of course, the other action that you could take is to not arrange a follow-on meeting with someone, even if they were one of your targets. For example, it's possible that it might pan out during the conversation that, for some reason or other, continuing to build that relationship with that person is not the most effective thing to do at that moment in time. They might, for example, already have someone in place doing what you do.

So there are valid reasons why you might not arrange a follow-on meeting. It's also a possibility that you will meet a lot of people at an event and it's physically not possible to meet up with all of them afterwards, so you'll have to choose.

At the Speed Networking events that I facilitate, I always clearly state the goals of the event for the attendees so that everyone understands the goals of the event, i.e. why we the event is being put on. Those goals are:

- *for everyone to meet everyone else there (I engineer this by a cunning, rotating seating plan for the attendees)*
- *as they meet everyone else, workout the people with whom they would like to follow up (it won't be everyone)*
- *make those follow-on arrangements*

By stating the goals at the beginning it helps to set the expectations with the attendees for what it is reasonable to achieve at the event (and also reminds them that they should be making follow-on arrangements!)

So when setting your SMART goals for the event, make sure you include follow-on meetings in those goals but be reasonable about how many you are aiming to achieve.

If your target audience is someone with whom you already have decent relationship, the goal might also be to arrange a follow-on meeting. However, it might be that your goal is just to carry on building that relationship. Perhaps you haven't seen them for a while and just want to catch up. Thinking back to **Joining the Dots**, your goal is simply to make their dot that little bit bigger.

What is your plan for approaching your target audience?

Now that you have identified who you want to talk to, spend a bit of time working out how you could go about that:

- Do you know them well? If so, grabbing them for a chat should not be difficult.
- Have you met them before but don't really know them? If so, you might need to remind them who you are and when you met before.
- Have you never met them? If so, who do you know who will be there who knows them and could maybe introduce you?

Of course, you could always just walk up to them and politely introduce yourself!

Whatever your approach, it's important to have a plan for whom you are going to approach and how.

Don't be afraid to ask people you know to introduce you to people you don't! Generally speaking, people who go networking want to introduce people to other people and get pleasure from doing so because they are helping somebody else. So don't deprive them of an opportunity to get some pleasure...

The final step in the creation of your target audience list is to prioritise it. Ideally, you would like to chat with all of your targets but circumstances might get in the way of that, particularly given the dynamic nature of most networking events. Adding priorities will help in maximising the effectiveness of your networking in these circumstances.

I have created a Target Audience Preparation Worksheet to help you with this planning. You can download that document from the Resources section on my website: www.intercog.co.uk.

As I mentioned a few moments ago, at the Speed Networking events that I facilitate, I use a cunning, rotating seating plan that ensures that all of the attendees meet all of the other attendees there. In effect, everyone gets a snippet of everyone else's time.

Using this orchestrated approach alleviates the need for attendees to work out who to approach and how to do it. This alleviates some stress and anxiety for people as many people find that aspect of networking a daunting prospect. Also, as everyone is using the same approach, it "levels the playing field" for everyone there and so novices as well as veterans can get a lot out of the event.

The way it works is also fun too!

NOTE: The prioritisation approach I mentioned above then comes into play when attendees are working out with whom they want to follow up and then making those arrangements after the "Speed" part of the event is completed.

What do you know about your target audience?

By working out your target audience you are ahead of those people that don't. Many people do create such a list but then they stop there. To be properly prepared, however, there is another step that needs to be done and that's to think some more about that audience.

Spend some time considering the following questions:

- What do you know about them, their business and their industry?
- What sort of person are they/do you expect them to be?
- What's important to them at the moment?
- What do you know about them outside the world of work?
- What do you need to find out from them?

There are more questions than these that you could consider but I'm sure you get the principle here!

And if you don't know the answers:

- Where could you find out?
- What research could you do?
- Who could you ask? (and could they introduce you?)

*In the **Social Media** part of this book I'll talk about people's online persona or presence. It's the sum total of everything that you can find out about them via the internet and, of course, some people's presence is larger and more active than others!*

Once you have considered these questions, then think about how you fit into the picture:

- What do/might they know about you?
- What might you need to tell them?
- How might you be able to help them?
- How might they be able to help you?

Again, there are many more questions that you could consider here.

Taking this audience-centric approach and doing this preparation is vital for achieving what you want at that event. Doing this for each and every event you attend will therefore increase the effectiveness of your networking as a whole.

In a moment I'll be looking more at the mechanics and skills on how to then put your plan into action. However, before I do that, there are a few final things to quickly address with regard to your audience.

What if your target audience isn't available?

If your target(s) aren't available to talk to, what do you do then?

There are a number of options here and the first one that often pops into someone's head is to grab something to eat or drink. And why not, it's there to be eaten and drunk after all!

The second option is to think back to your plan and how you were going to approach your target(s). If the plan were to ask someone you know to introduce you then is that person free? If so, now is the time to chat to them and then casually drop into the conversation your desire to chat to your target and ask if they could introduce you.

And the third option is to chat to anybody who is free. Yes, anybody!

Now I know what you're thinking: Doesn't that go against the whole "you need to target to be effective" concept?

Well, not really, for the following reasons:

- You're not doing this all of the time, only when needs must because your target(s) are not free.
- Doing nothing is not effective and so you might as well be doing something.
- You don't know who you don't know. They *might* turn out to be really interesting and/or a contact with great potential.
- You don't know who you don't know **knows**. Perhaps they could make some great introductions.
- It's good to practise!

If this happens, just talk to somebody, anybody. It's OK, you're allowed!

If you are talking to somebody who is not your target, don't be too quick to dismiss them as not being useful and never give them the impression that they are just a time filler or stepping-stone to somebody else. The key to effective networking is relationships and so they need to be built properly, and politely, with whomever you are talking.

Do you actually need to take a targeted approach?

The next thing to quickly address is whether or not you have to take a targeted approach for every networking event. I suspect that you are expecting me to say that you do but in fact you don't (with a caveat).

You don't have to take a targeted approach at *every* networking event you go to. On occasion, it's actually quite refreshing just to go along and see what happens. It will give you the opportunity to practise some of the tips and techniques I'll mention later in this framework without the "pressure" of having to do it with your target(s).

The key words though are *on occasion*. The majority of the time your networking activities need to be targeted to be productive.

Is it OK to just talk to people you know?

The final thing I'm going to do in this section is to ask you the same question I enjoy asking the people I work with when I'm training or coaching them:

> Is it OK to go to a networking event and *only* talk to people that you *already* know?

What do you think - is it?

How would you answer that question?

When I have asked this question in the past, it often leads to puzzled looks on some of their faces. "So you're asking us if it is OK to go to a networking event and to not meet anyone new?", they often reply. "Doesn't that go against the core purpose of networking which is to meet new people and make more contacts?"

On first glance it would appear that it does. However, it actually doesn't.

The core purpose of networking is to develop relationships, both new and *existing*. Talking to people you already know is a way of building, and deepening, those existing relationships. So talking to people you already know is an essential part of building a strong network and has a direct effect on how successful your networking activities will therefore be.

But:

- if you are going to do this, then that needs to be your plan, your objective for that event
- you can't just do this all of the time or your network won't get any bigger

So it is OK, on occasion, just to focus on increasing the size of some of the dots in your network.

RA**I**L

So I've covered "why" and "who", let's now take a look at "how".

The **I** here stands for "Be **interested** and be **interesting**."

There are two parts to this and the order is important.

Be Interested

Firstly, you need to be interested in your audience, the other people there.

Dale Carnegie is quoted as saying (words to the effect of): "People are interested in people who are interested in them."

It sounds a bit odd but it is true. The more you are interested in someone, the more you appear interesting to *them*.

So what's the best way to be interested in them? What's the easiest way of finding things out about them?

Ask questions!

With only a bit of practice it will become an easy thing to do and that's partly because there are so many questions that you could ask.

I have created an Audience Questions Preparation Worksheet to help you with this planning. You can download that document from the Resources section on my website: www.intercog.co.uk.

If you want to, take a moment at this point to download the worksheet and blast as many questions as you can think of into it. You'll be surprised how many you can think of once you get going! (Even if you don't do it now, make sure you do before an event)

In the worksheet, I suggest categories of questions relating to your audience and considering:

- their business
- their role
- what they do
- their clients/customers
- their successes
- their challenges
- them as a person

There are no doubt other questions and categories that you can think of as well!

 *In his book "The Jelly Effect", Andy Bounds recommends asking the BIG QUESTION: "What professions are good contacts for you?". In other words, "Who would you most like to be introduced to?" In either form it's a great question and one I'll refer back to a couple of times later in this book.*

These are all generic questions and are great stock questions to have thought about before going networking and then have at the ready for when you are there.

On an event by event basis, as part of your preparation you can then also add some specific questions that are focussed on your target(s). This extra level of specificness will make your target(s) feel more special as it shows that you are taking an increased amount of interest in them, which will consequently make you appear to be even more interesting in their eyes too.

Asking questions, though is only part of the story. What you also need to do is listen to their answers. In fact, you need to *actively* listen to their answers.

So what does *actively* listen mean?

It means that listening is a two-way activity that you take a part in as well. You are actively doing things whilst you are listening to maximise the effectiveness of that conversation. You are not just "sitting back" and hearing the words.

Active listening involves:
- giving your audience your full attention
    - outwardly showing an interest with things like:
        - appropriate eye contact
        - nodding
        - verbal continuation clues:
            - u-huh
            - OK
            - go on
    - using their name
    - not letting your attention drift to other people in the room (that you would like to speak to later perhaps)
- letting them go first
- letting them finish what they are saying
    - not interrupting
    - not finishing their sentences for them
    - not talking over them
    - letting them tell their whole story
        - don't jump to assumptions/conclusions
        - don't offer advice too soon

- providing reflective input
    - paraphrasing
    - summarising
    - parroting what they have said
- asking appropriate follow-on questions
    - make references to their previous answers in those questions

 *Don't underestimate the power of a pause, the power of not speaking. So when they appear to have stopped talking, just look them in the eye and pause for a moment. If they have got more to say then they will carry on. This cycle will continue until they really have run out of things to say at that point of the conversation. Although it sounds slightly paradoxical, well used silence will help to keep the conversation going!*

So it's a cycle:
1. Ask a question
2. Actively listen to their answer
3. Go to step 1

Using this approach is a great way of learning about your audience, potentially both on a business and a personal level. What it also does is allow you to work out their priorities and their needs which in turn will allow you to work out who it might be useful for you to introduce them to.

*In the **HELPful Introduction** Framework I'll go into more detail about how this can be done and what can be done as part of your normal networking activities to allow it to be done more easily.*

The other benefit of taking this approach is that it solves the "I don't know what to say when I'm networking" problem. When I'm working with people who are looking to get more out of their networking they often cite this as one of their issues. They feel nervous about joining a group of people because they don't know what to say. This questions-based approach can take away that problem as you can effectively work out what to say before going because you can create a set of questions you can ask. By asking those questions of your audience first it also allows you to ease into the conversation and to relax a bit in the process.

Be Interesting

At some point though, it will be your turn to talk and that's where the second part of this step in the framework comes into play: "Be interesting".

So I'd like to extend Dale Carnegie's quote: "People are interested in people who are interested in them. But it's a lot easier to be interested in someone if they are interesting in the first place!"

If you think of the people that you meet at networking events then you will know that there is a spectrum of "interestingness" from the dull as dishwater bores at one end to the charismatic life and souls of the party at the other end.

In reality though, anyone can be interesting, yes anyone! All it takes is planning and practice. And most of it is in the planning.

So let's think about that planning for a moment. You are going to be asked questions at a networking event. So what might you be asked?

I have created a Self-Questions Preparation Worksheet to help you with this planning. You can download that document from the Resources section on my website: www.intercog.co.uk.

As before, feel free to take a moment at this point to download the worksheet and blast as many questions as you can think of into it.

In the worksheet, I again suggested categories of questions but this time they are relating to you and:

- your business
- your role
- what you do
- your clients/customers
- your successes
- your challenges
- you as a person

As before, there are no doubt other questions and categories that you can think of as well.

*One of the most common questions you will be asked is "What do you do?". You will probably be asked this very near the beginning of the conversation and so it's crucially important to get off to a good start with an interesting answer. The **ICE** Framework goes into more detail on how to do this.*

The great thing is that you can predict what you might be asked ahead of the event so you can work out in advance of the event what your answers for those questions might be. If you know what you are going to talk about, which you will do if you work out the answers in advance, then you can take confidence from remembering that while you are at the event.

*Taking a moment to remember that you are prepared and ready is something that I'll come back to in more detail in the **PROWESS** Framework.*

As you are working out your answers to these questions, think of incorporating into those answers:

- how you help people
- what differences you make to people
- the problems you solve
- the solutions you provide
- the benefits you bring
- examples of what you have done
- stories that you can tell

And don't forget the BIG QUESTION I mentioned earlier: Who would you most like to be introduced to? Make sure you have some good answers for that one, answers that you might also vary accordingly to whom you are speaking at the time.

Your goal with your answers is to help people to understand what you do, either for their own benefit or for the benefit of their contacts.

*Again, in the **HELPful Introduction** Framework I'll go into more detail about this and why it's so important for others to understand how you help people.*

With this "bank" of answers you are then ready for the questions that you will be asked. Don't deliver them verbatim though as that will take you towards the wrong end of the "interestingness" spectrum. Use them as a guide and answer naturally and with an appropriate amount of passion. Where possible, incorporate into your answers information that you have gleaned from your audience's answers as this will reinforce the impression of the high level of interest you have taken in them. You can only do this if they have gone first though which is another reason why it's better to let them go first.

Over time, and with practice, you will get better at relating your key information to your audience and being interesting whilst doing it too!

Also, whilst you are in "answer mode", don't be afraid to ask questions as well. Asking questions is a great way of finding out how what you do relates to what your audience does, or what they need. Asking them how you might be able to help them specifically can be potentially very rewarding as long as it's done politely and genuinely and not in any sort of pushy or salesy way.

The last thing to say in this section is just to briefly mention the two, hopefully obvious, components of question answering etiquette:

- listen to the question in full, i.e. don't start answering the question until it has been asked in its entirety
- answer the question you are asked

Nobody likes being interrupted when they are asking a question or people not answering the question they have asked or people answering the question they thought they were going to be asked when they jumped in half-way through it being asked!

In mitigation to the above, many people find networking events scary and the extra stress this causes them might lead to them jumping in excitedly without realising that they are, sticking to a prepared answer even if it doesn't quite fit what they'd been asked or seizing the opportunity to answer a question that they think they are in the process of being asked because they know they can answer that question.

The simple steps to counter this are:

- be prepared
- remember that you are prepared and take confidence from it
- let them ask the question
- answer the question you have been asked

Simples!

At the Speed Networking events that I facilitate, there are a number of rounds of networking. In each round, attendees are sitting at a table that also has a facilitator and in every round the facilitator asks those people at their table two questions that they then answer in turn.

Using this approach works well, not only because it is structured and controlled by the facilitator (so everyone gets to have their say) but also because it has all of the benefits of the questions-based approach described above.

RAI**L**

The last step in this framework is all about **Logistics** and the things that need to be considered before, during and after the event.

Some of this isn't rocket science but it is all important!

Before the Event

There are a number of things that you need to consider before the event:

- timings:
    - What date is the event?
    - When does it start?
    - When do you want to arrive?

- location:
    - How long will it take to get there?
    - What will the traffic be like?
    - Where can you park?
    - Do you have to pay for parking?
- dress code:
    - What is the appropriate/expected/required attire for the event?
- food and drink:
    - Will there be any?
    - Have you notified the hosts of any dietary requirements?
    - Do you eat before you go?

The other thing to consider is what to take with you.

It is at this point in my training courses that I challenge the learners to correctly identify the seven things that I suggest to always take to networking events.

So what do you think that they are?

Here's my list:
1. Pen
2. Spare pen
3. Notepad
4. Business cards
5. Mints/breath freshener
6. Diary (this is potentially your phone)
7. Badge

You might be surprised by this last item.

Why would you want to take a badge? Surely they'll give you one at the event won't they?

They probably will but taking one of your own as a backup is a sensible thing to do just in case they don't. Having your own badge also works around the following issues:
- the hosts missed you off the delegate list and so need to hand-write you one:
    - there's nothing like a hand-written badge to scream "last-minute" or "bad organisation"
    - a hand-written badge will not help to make a great first impression
- there is a typo on the badge they have created
- their badge is badly designed and hard to read

- they have just given you the plastic holder and are expecting you to put your business card in it to act as a badge
    - business cards make bad badges as the text is normally far too small to be read
    - this really doesn't work well either for those of us with portrait business cards!
- their badge doesn't look as professional as the one you have taken with you (which you have probably paid to have made)

And just to finish off about badges, here's a question for you. Where do you wear it?

Most people (and perhaps you too) answer with something that equates to "on the left-hand side of the chest". So it might be on a lapel or a pocket for example. It's not a surprising answer really as there is often a lapel or pocket right there that seems tailor-made for the badge (pun intended). Add to that the fact that most people are right-handed then it's the easiest place to put it.

Sadly, it's also the wrong place!

For maximum impact and effect, your badge should be worn on the right-hand side of your chest. That's because it is easier to read and generally more accessible when you shake hands with other people. A badge on the right of your chest is much more in the other person's eyeline than if it were on the left. In fact, depending on the angle at which you approach each other, the badge might not even be visible at all if worn on the left!

To see the difference the positioning of a badge can make, have a look at the video about this that can be found in the Resources section of my website: www.intercog.co.uk.

But why does that matter? Surely people will say their name when they introduce themselves?

Perhaps, but not always. There's also the possibility of:
- them only saying their first name
- there being a lot of background noise
- people having soft or gentle voices
- hearing impediments
- unusual names that are hard to grasp at first hearing
- (they haven't read this book)

Being able to see a name badge in these circumstances really will help with making a great first impression. By wearing your badge on the right you are also helping them in the above circumstances and they will appreciate that help (even if they don't realise what you've done or say "thanks" for doing it).

One of my connections, Richard, and I have a running private joke in that he always reckons that, when he's at a networking event, he can work out who I have coached or trained (or haven't) because they are wearing their badge on the right (not the left).

As a final thought on what to take with you, one thing I haven't mentioned above is any sales or marketing collateral and that's because whether or not to take these very much depends on the type and format of the event itself. For those events where there is a place to display your collateral or there is the expectation that it will be given out, then clearly you should take it. However, not all events are like that and so careful consideration needs to be made when deciding when to take it into an event. (You can potentially take it and leave it in the car just in case, for example).

It many ways it's about perception. Somebody wandering round with lots of sales and marketing material by default gives off an air of a "salesperson" and, as I said earlier, networking is not about selling. People don't like being sold to at a networking event, especially if the material is given out without asking permission, in the same way that some people feel the need to deal out business cards, which is something I'll come back to in a moment.

At the Speed Networking events that I facilitate, I set aside a table which I refer to as the "collateral table". At the start of the event I request that the attendees put their business cards, flyers, sales collateral etc onto that table. I then actively dissuade them from giving anything out during the "Speed" part of the event and reaffirm that their collateral will be there for all to see and take later in the event.

This allows the attendees to focus on what the other attendees are saying without "collateral damage" to that focus and makes for a more effective event.

During the Event

When you arrive at an event, the first thing to do is to take a moment to see who is there. So before approaching anyone, take a moment to survey the scene. This will help you with the execution of your plan to meet your target audience.

Then, there are only really three steps to the process of networking at an event:

1. Work out which group you can/want to join
2. Join the group and have a conversation
3. Leave the group

(if there is time left, go to step 1)

Let's look at each in turn.

1. Work out which group you can/want to join

As you are looking around the room, work out which groups you can approach. There are two types of groups: open and closed. Open groups will have a gap in them where it is possible for someone to join that group. Closed groups don't.

And then there's somebody who is standing on their own. What do you think they are thinking? Most probably, it's something along the lines of "I wish someone would come and talk to me!". So somebody standing on their own is effectively an open group by default.

I have created a video which looks at open and closed groups in more detail with examples of how they appear in practice. You can access that video via the Resources section of my website: www.intercog.co.uk.

So as far as working out which groups you can join, only approach open groups. It really is as simple as that!

If all of the groups are closed, which is highly unlikely, simply wait, grab something to eat or drink or peruse the delegate list. It won't be long before a group opens up.

2. Join the group

First things first, be patient. It might take a few minutes for a group to open up.

Once it's open, politely approach the gap in the group and wait to be invited to join. Most often, the group will see you approaching and there will be a natural pause in the conversation as they ask you to join. If they don't ask you to join in that pause, politely ask if you could join. It's unlikely they will say no as it was an open group. (If the people in the group don't want to be joined they will subconsciously create a closed group)

Then join the group by stepping into the space and doing the normal introductions, handshakes etc.

*I talk more about how to make a glowing first impression later in this book when I talk about the **SHINE** Framework.*

Then respect the pre-existing nature of the group and the conversation and wait to join in the conversation. And then, be interested and be interesting!

3. Leave the group
For a variety of reasons you might want to leave that group and move on.

As you do:
- agree/reiterate any follow-on actions
- thank them for their time
- wish them an enjoyable "rest of event"
- shake hands
- (go!)

You will do the same steps as well (except the last one) when somebody else leaves the group (but you don't).

Sometimes, however, it's not quite so easy to leave a group, especially if you have "got lumbered with a bore". You get stuck with the person that goes on and on about stuff that's not interesting or relevant to you and they are using up your precious time when you'd rather be talking to one of your targets.

It has happened to me and I'm guessing it has happened to you too!

What do you do? What do you say? How do you end the conversation politely and professionally?

So when this has happened to you in the past, what did you do, what did you say?
(If you are lucky enough to have not had this happen to you, then what options can you think of to get out of this situation?)

When I have asked this question on my courses I often get the answer, "Oh excuse me, I need to go to the toilet/bathroom or for a comfort break etc".

It's a common ploy and might work but runs the risk of back-firing if they say, "Good idea. I'll go too!". Then you are *really* stuck with them…

There is a better, more sure-fire way of politely and professionally escaping a bore and it comes back to THE BIG QUESTION I mentioned earlier: Who would you most like to be introduced to?

If, during the conversation, you have ascertained who that is for the person you are stuck with, you can then use it to your advantage as part of an "escape clause" like this:

> *So, if I remember correctly, you were interested in being introduced to HR Directors. Yes?*
>
> *Well I've enjoyed our chat and I'm guessing you want to meet lots of people here too.*

So, as I chat to the others here I'll keep an eye out for you for any HR Directors.

Enjoy the rest of the event!

In essence, what you are implying is that you are offering to do some referral marketing and networking connection building on their behalf. Very few people are going to say no to that offer.

So those are the three simple steps to networking during an event. Before moving on to look at what needs to be done after the event, there are a couple of things just to cover off: business cards and refreshments.

If someone at a networking event thrusts their business card towards you uninvited, how does it make you feel? What impression to they make on you?

Now I can't read your mind to know exactly what your answers were to those two questions but I'd hazard a guess that they would not have been positive.

Very few people like a "dealer". If nothing else, it shows a lack of respect to the person on the receiving end of the card. It's also a waste of money for the person dealing the cards as they'll spend a lot more money getting so many cards printed.

So choose to whom you would like to give your business cards. Have a legitimate mutual purpose for giving one out and, before doing so, ask if you can give them your card, it's only polite to do so.

It's rare that somebody will refuse your card as they will either actually want it or will politely accept it as it's easier to do that than reject it. You will save money this way too! And if someone gives you a business card, make sure that you thank them and pay it some attention. Don't just stick it straight into your pocket.

The other things that you will need to manage during an event are the refreshments. Fortunately, I've got a whole framework for that later in the book!

*The **Thought for Food** Framework will cover the best ways to juggle food and drink at an event without negatively impacting those that you are talking to. (Don't take the references to juggling and impacting literally though!)*

After the Event
Do what you said you were going to do, when you said you were going to, with whom you said you were going to do it.

That's the key to what to do after the event!

In some circumstances you can do even more than you said you would. There are potentially things that you could send to them that you had not discussed or mentioned. Examples are:

- free materials and resources
- links to relevant information on the internet
- invitations to other events
- recommendations for connections and introductions

As long as what is offered is well meant, useful and not "spammy" then it can work positively in building that relationship. Sending them this "bonus" information is also a way of keeping in touch which it is important to do as building the relationship will take time.

*In addition to simply emailing people, Social Media can be used to disseminate your "useful stuff" to your contacts. I'll talk more about the specifics of this later in **Part 4** where I talk about Social Media.*

It's also worth keeping/recording the information on your contacts in your filing mechanism of choice. How much information you keep, how detailed it is and how much you actively use it is very much down to you. Suffice it to say that it's a great store of information that can assist with your future planning and goal setting. Don't forget the legalities around storing this sort of data, however…

Recap

Putting it all together, here's a summary of the **RAIL** Framework:

What are your **R**easons for going?
Focus on your (target) **A**udience
Be **I**nterested and be Interesting
What are the **L**ogistics? (before, during and after)

Online Considerations

Let's look at each step in turn.

What are your Reasons for going?

You still need to know why you are attending this online event!

Focus on your (target) Audience

Working our who your target audience is before you go to the event is still a good approach if it's an online event. You can still use the same techniques for segmenting and targeting as you would for an in-person event.

One of the benefits of an online networking event is that it potentially nullifies geographical restrictions. Whilst you wouldn't consider going to a two-hour networking event in Australia if you were based in the UK, you might consider attending an online version of that event (although you might need to set an alarm clock!). Online events mean that your potential audience is now a LOT bigger...

For an online event you might still be emailed a delegate list prior to the event in the same way that you might for an in-person event. However, if this doesn't happen there are some disadvantages of not being physically at the event. The first is that you can't be given a physical delegate list. The second is that you can't discreetly look at the name badges when you arrive.

One of the other big differences for an online event is that how much information a delegate shares with other online attendees is controlled by them personally. So if the delegate just decides to display a name of "Dave", with no surname or company for example, it's harder to know who they are.

Some people use the same technology for business and personal events and some of those technologies remember the last name that was used. Watch out for this. It's never a good idea to turn up at a business networking event as "Quiz Team Aguilera" or "The Famous Five".

It's good practice therefore to always show your full name at least when you are online. Also, if the technology has the capability, if the event etiquette allows or if the organisers request it, you could add your company name to your name that is displayed and/or put your company and/or contact details into a chat window for example. How much information you can display and where you display it varies between technologies and so the general rule of thumb is to show as much as you can whilst still being in keeping with the event, its etiquette and the technology.

In addition, some technologies allow you to save the contents of a chat window (or equivalent) during the event and so that is one way that you can get people's contact details. You could also ask the organisers to send them out after the event too.

Be Interested and be Interesting

Everything in this section also applies to online networking.

One thing that's true though is that it's generally harder to have a conversation between a number of people online than it is in person. This is probably due to a combination of people being more practiced at doing it in person and there being more visual and non-verbal clues present in person than when online.

That means that it's even more important to be a competent active listener online if you want to make the most out of those conversations.

What are the Logistics? (before, during and after)
Before
What you do before the event is very different if it's an online event.

You clearly still need to "arrive" on time although there will be no travel time. That being said, make sure you have tested your technology in good time prior to the event so it does not delay your joining the event.

Although you don't actually need to take anything with you to the event, it is handy to have a way of making notes and booking things into your diary. Giving somebody a physical business card is also not possible but you do need to be ready to give them your contact details electronically if asked via the most appropriate route available. So be ready to do that.

What you wear is still important so that you make the correct impression (although some people would argue that you only need to dress in business attire from the waist up!) Beware of wearing fancy patterns and checks, though, as they can sometimes create weird interference with some cameras.

Perhaps the biggest difference with an online event is that you are in control of your own environment. It is therefore down to you how you present your surroundings when online and that is something that you will need to get set up in advance of the event. You therefore need to consider your:

- camera
    - make sure your camera is at eye level
    - fill the screen (make it personal)
    - talk to the camera (not the other faces on your screen)
    - when using a phone/tablet, prop the device up to reduce camera movement
- background
    - make sure there is nothing distracting/offensive behind you, e.g.:
        - static things (like posters, messiness etc)
        - other people or things moving (inside or outside)
            - close doors/draw curtains/blinds if required
    - if necessary, cover or hide things, e.g.:
        - use a backdrop but make sure how you cover things does not make things look worse!
    - possibly use a virtual background if the technology permits
        - choose an appropriate (non-distracting) background
        - beware of causing unexpected effects due to you or your clothes clashing with the background
    - used carefully and correctly, though, your background can be used as a talking point or a conversation starter as well as a means of providing more "interesting" information to your audience

- lighting
    - make sure you are well lit
    - the light needs to be in front of you not behind
        - don't sit with a window/bright light behind you
    - use lights to fill in or add light as required
        - use "soft" lighting where possible
    - avoid lighting your face from only one side
        - use lights to lighten the dark side
    - alternatively, draw the curtains/blinds to shut out the light and add controlled light
- sound
    - make sure your microphone captures your voice clearly and is crackle/echo free
    - consider which sort of microphone you need to use:
        - laptop, webcam, lapel/clip-on, stand alone, headphone?
    - consider which speakers to use:
        - laptop, computer, headphones, earphones/pods?
    - consider the impression each of the above makes to the other participants
    - remove/reduce background noise
        - use a noise cancelling microphone
        - choose a quiet location
        - let people around you know you are attending an online event and ask them to be quiet
- furniture
    - make sure your working environment is comfortable

Assuming the technology allows, it's very rare for someone to not display their video at an online networking event as people expect to see faces in the same way they do at an in-person event. However, there are some legitimate reasons for someone to not display their video (e.g. because of a very distracting background, respecting privacy etc) but not being bothered (with things like attire, hair, shaving and/or makeup etc) isn't one of those reasons...

The final thing to consider is that the other people at the event can only see what your camera shows them. You can therefore have other things that can help you out of sight. These might be other windows on your screen, a second screen, reference sheets on your desk etc. So you could for example have:
- your website visible (for reference)
- websites displayed for your target(s)
- news articles displayed
- your completed sheets from your preparation
- etc

Whilst you don't want your focus (and eye contact) to be drawn away from those with whom you are chatting, surreptitious referencing of this "hidden" information can help to make a great impression and have an effective networking style.

During
The biggest difference during the event is over the control you may or may not have over who you can talk to. When you are there in person at an event you can pretty much go where you would like to and talk to whoever you want to, politeness and openness considered of course. With an online event, however, it is possible that you don't have any, or as much, control over who you can meet at that event.

*Because you may have no or little control over who you can talk to it makes it even more important to remember your purpose and be outgoing. I'll come back to this in the online considerations for the **PROWESS** Framework.*

Once you are in a group chatting, however, the same principles apply regarding that conversation as for an in-person event.

With regard to food and drink, that's totally in your control so think carefully what you will eat or drink during the event. Although it might only lead to your own mouse getting sticky, it's probably best not to eat during the event if possible. Having a drink nearby is a good idea though.

After
After the event you need to follow up in the same way as you would for an in-person event.

The ICE Framework

For helping you to get off to an interesting start.

Earlier in this book in the **RAIL** Framework, I talked about the need for you to be interesting to your audience and that it takes preparation and practice to do so (for some more than others admittedly).

The **ICE** Framework is a three-step process for creating an interesting impression right from the start of the conversation, right from that very first question "What do you do?".

Think of it as an interesting way of breaking the ice. (These acronyms don't just make themselves up you know!)

*In his book "The Jelly Effect", Andy Bounds talks about his concept of AFTERS which helps people to focus on how they help other people or, in other words, how those other people are different afterwards. He also covers how the AFTERS approach can be used to good effect during introductions. I mention it here because reading Andy's book provided the spark for my **ICE** Framework.*

ICE

You won't be surprised that the I here stands for **Interest**, or more precisely, **Create Interest**.

The goal is to get a response along the lines of:

- Well that sounds interesting.
- Tell me more.
- How do you do that then?

The goal is also to do it in a single sentence so you're instantly interesting.

However, before I talk about how you can do this, let's take a look at how someone might introduce themself at a networking event.

You: "So what do you do?"

Them: "I'm an accountant."

It's not the most interesting of replies is it? And it also doesn't differentiate them from any other accountants who might be at the event either.

 *I've only used an accountant here as it allows me to use a particular, easily understood example in a few moments. I'm not trying to imply that accountants are boring. I know many interesting accountants!*

The accountant hasn't told you what they do, they've just told you their job title. In fact, that happens a lot at networking events:

- I'm a business coach
- I'm a plumber
- I'm a managing director
- etc

So how could it be done better?

Very simply.

Think about what you do and how you help people.

Then when you get asked what you do, answer with a single sentence that starts with the words "I help" and ends with how you help people.

It's probable that you help people in many different ways and so you have multiple ways that you could end that sentence. That gives you the ability to choose an ending that best fits with your audience and be even more interesting to them.

So let's go back to our accountant example:

> You: "So what do you do?"
>
> Them: "I help people to pay less tax, legally of course, so they can spend their hard-earned money on what they want to rather than give it to the Government."

Now they sound more like somebody you would like to talk to!

When you start to think about what you do in this way you can come up with some very interesting and different answers and so I would encourage you to explore in more detail how you help people. Think of different ways you could answer that question and for each answer that you come up with ask:

- and how does that help them?
- and what does that mean that they can now do?
- and what difference does that make and to whom?

And then ask those same questions again for your new set of answers.

When you start really looking at how people are different after you have done what you do, then you can come up with some really interesting ways of answering the question: "What do you do?".

> In the **HELPful Introduction** Framework I talk about how it's much easier to introduce people if you know how they help other people. Using the **ICE** Framework will clearly help with making those introductions.

I**C**E

The next thing to do is to **provide some Context** to position and explain a little bit more about what you do. This is where you might introduce some of the "pain" points that you address because of how you help people. You're still not saying a lot but you are saying more than you did in the previous step.

So let's go back to our accountant example:

You: "So what do you do?"

Them: "I help people to pay less tax, legally of course, so they can spend their hard-earned money on what they want to rather than give it to the Government."

You: "Now that sounds like something I'd want! How do you do it?"

Them: "Well there are so many taxes out there: Income Tax, VAT, Corporation Tax, Dividend Tax, Capital Gains Tax and many more. Most people don't really understand them but we do. So we look at all of the taxes that someone is paying and work out the best ways that they can legally pay less tax so they'll have more money left over to spend on what they want to."

The goal is to flush out a bit more of what you do and to entice the audience to want to know more. It's probable that they then might ask something along the lines of, "So who have you done that for?" and that nicely leads into the third step.

IC**E**

The final thing to do is to then **expand with Examples**. Tell them for whom you have done what you do and, in tangible terms that your audience will understand, how you have helped them. You need to use examples to which they will relate so they can start working out if you can help them too.

As the old adage goes, "Facts tell. Stories sell!" This is where you tell them those stories, stories that are memorable and will differentiate you from the others there who might have similar offerings to you.

Finishing off our accountant example then:

> You: "So what do you do?"
>
> Them: "I help people to pay less tax, legally of course, so they can spend their hard-earned money on what they want to rather than give it to the Government."
>
> You: "Now that sounds like something I'd want! How do you do it?"
>
> Them: "Well there are so many taxes out there: Income Tax, VAT, Corporation Tax, Dividend Tax, Capital Gains Tax and many more. Most people don't really understand them but we do. So we look at all of the taxes that someone is paying and work out the best ways that they can legally pay less tax so they'll have more money left over to spend on what they want to."
>
> You: "Sounds like a great help! So who've you done that for then?
>
> Them: "One of our clients is a Director for a local, profitable printing company. He wasn't sure but he had an idea he was paying too much tax and so asked us in to have a look. As it turned out, he was indeed paying more tax than he could have been. So we investigated the options and ended up saving him enough money to take his family to Disney for a week. Everyone ended up happy!"

But don't go on too long in this third step. You are now properly entering into a conversation and that needs to be bi-directional and not just you doing the talking. Keep that conversation balanced between all parties.

So next time someone asks you "What do you do?", break the **ICE**!

*I have created a worksheet that will help you to put the **ICE** Framework into practice. You can download it from the Resources section of my website: www.intercog.co.uk.*

Recap

Putting it all together, here's a summary of the **ICE** Framework:

Create **I**nterest
Provide a **C**ontext
Expand with **E**xamples

Online Considerations

The **ICE** Framework works equally well online as it does in person.

Part 3

How to be Confident at Networking Events

Much of the groundwork for being confident whilst networking is done by being prepared to go networking (i.e. what's in Part 2).

All you need to do now is to go networking with confidence. It's all you need to do...

And that's also easier said than done!

However, thinking back to the **CAPS** Framework, your confidence will be building because you have been doing your **Preparation** and thinking about your **Audience**.

This part of the book will therefore focus more on the **Skills** side of things. Some of this will be about adopting positive mindsets and ways of thinking and some of this will be about actual tips, tricks and techniques that you can use to network more confidently and therefore more effectively.

The Confidence Cycle

For helping you to know where to start in being more confident when going networking.

There are lots of different theories about where to start when trying to be more confident when you are networking with other people.

For me, the place to start is very simply to know how to *look* like you are confident.

If you look like you are confident, people will think that you are confident.

If people think that you are confident, they will treat you as if you are confident.

If they treat you as if you are confident, then that will make you feel more confident.

If you feel more confident, then you'll start to look even more confident.

And so the cycle continues – it's the Confidence Cycle!

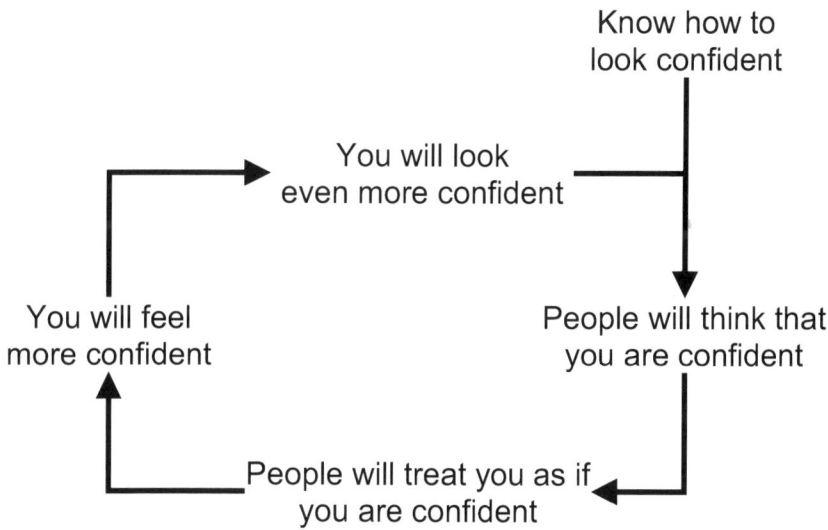

So the place to start your confidence building journey is to learn the tips, tricks and techniques about how to *look* like you are confident. And that's what the following frameworks are primarily all about!

Online Considerations

The Confidence Cycle applies regardless of the type of networking event.

The PROWESS Framework

For helping you to exude confidence when networking.

After the obligatory Magnifier app (because I'm getting old and everything needs to be that little bit bigger), the second app I installed on my new phone was a Thesaurus (as I like to do puzzles). That app defines "prowess" as:

> ability, skill and bravery

And that's exactly what this framework is aiming for with regard to your attending a networking event.

The **PROWESS** Framework is a seven-part acronymic guide. Each of the letters represents one tip, trick or technique to help you to look confident whilst you are networking. And if you *look* confident…

The first two letters (PR) are things to remember just before you enter the event.

The next two letters (OW) relate to aspects of the mindset to have whilst you are there.

And the last three letters (ESS) are physical things that you can do to project a confident and capable demeanour.

Let's examine each letter in turn.

PROWESS

Firstly, **remember your Purpose**.

Having a clear purpose for a networking event is something I stressed earlier in this book as being hugely important in being effective while networking. I suggested that you spent time working out what that purpose was as part of your preparing for the event.

Now picture yourself about to enter the event. Take a moment to remind yourself and to remember what your purpose is and keep that purpose near the focus of your thoughts whilst you are there. It's possible that you might get distracted from it and go off on a few unrelated tangents or activities but if you keep an eye on your purpose then you can return back to it more readily. You are much more likely to be more successful at that event if you do this.

pROWESS

The R in the **PROWESS** Framework is to **(remember that you) are Ready**.

Remember that you is in brackets so I'll come back to that later.

It's a fairly obvious thing to say but if you are ready, if you have done your preparation, then your networking will go better!

There is a clear link here back to the **CAPS** Framework where the **P** stood for **Preparation**. The more prepared you are, the more ready you are, the more confident you will look and feel. So all of the preparation that I talked about earlier in the book in the **RAIL** and **ICE** Frameworks will stand you in good stead when you get to the event.

Whilst it's important to be ready, the thing here that actually gives the confidence boost is that bit in the brackets – to *remember that you* are ready.

Let me give you an example of what I mean.

Imagine that next week you have a Maths test and that passing this test is massively important to you. There are ten questions on the test and you need to get six questions correct in order to pass the test. Fortunately (and legitimately) you have today been given six of the questions from next week's test.

What are you going to do between now and the test next week?

You'll work out the answers to those six questions - obviously!

You're doing your preparation, or in other words, you're getting ready.

Now imagine yourself standing outside the examination room next week. How will you be feeling?

You'll probably be feeling a little nervous but you'll also be feeling more confident about taking the test because you know six of the answers already. In fact, if you take a conscious moment to stop and think about that fact, that you are ready, you'll feel even more confident.

And that's the key!

Yes, you need to be prepared but it's the taking a moment to reflect on the fact that you are ready that gives you that extra confidence boost.

So take a moment before entering the networking event to remember that you are ready…

PR**O**WESS

The first element of a confident mindset whilst networking is to **be Outgoing**.

Not an "in your face" or annoyingly loud outgoing of course. It's more of the fact that you need to accept that you will need to potentially go and talk to other people and so be outgoing. Networking, by its very nature, needs you to do this if you want to achieve your purpose. You can't rely on people approaching you all of the time (although it will happen that way round some of the time).

If you are of an outgoing nature anyway, then this will not be too much of an issue for you. If, however, you have more of an introverted personality, you will find this harder to do. It will take more courage to do this (which is why I liked the fact that my app included "bravery" in the definition of prowess).

Various topics that I have covered so far in this book will help with that courage, for example:

- having a purpose
- identifying your targets and "researching" them
- working out how to approach them and what to say when you get there (which will be different for each person)
- knowing how to be interested and interesting
- recognising which groups you can approach (and which you can't)
- taking confidence from remembering that you have done all of the above

I know – you could argue that all of the above will help naturally outgoing people too and you'd be right!

So you need to be outgoing and you can be – you have the knowledge and skills to do it…

PRO**W**ESS

The second aspect of a confident mindset to have whilst networking is to **be Welcoming**.

You may well know from personal experience how nerve-racking it can be to approach a group of strangers at a networking event and also what difference it makes to you if you are warmly welcomed when you join the group. It really helps to settle the nerves and accelerates the speed with which you can then join in with the conversation.

In such a circumstance, how does it make you feel about those who have welcomed you?

You are probably going to be thankful to them and your perceptions of them will be positive. They will have made a good first impression on you.

So flip it round the other way. Imagine you are now the one who is welcoming the newcomer to the group. Consider their thoughts about you by warmly welcoming them and the impression that you are making on them. Why would you not want to do that? (That's a rhetorical question by the way!)

Compare the above to a group that is unwelcoming and the first impressions that they would make...

So, where possible or appropriate, engineer your group to be an open one, with a gap, so people can join you. If you see people approaching the group, at the opportune moment, invite them into the group and, again at the opportune moment, invite them into the conversation. (Fortunately, you have a host of tailor-made questions to allow you to do that!)

They will thank you for doing this, perhaps not audibly, but certainly mentally and at some point they will want to return that favour.

There are some occasions when you don't want to be joined by others at a networking event. You might be engaged in private or business-related conversations that are only for the ears of those already present in the group. In this case you can put up a polite "Do not Disturb" sign by making your group closed, i.e. without any gaps. That in itself should deter people from trying to join you.

PROW**E**SS

The E in the **PROWESS** Framework is all about **maintaining appropriate Eye contact**.

When you're having a conversation with someone, the best way to engage with that person is to look them in the eye as direct eye contact draws people into the conversation. The person that you are looking at feels like you are giving them your personal focus and that, at that moment, they have all of your attention.

It also takes a certain amount of confidence to look someone in the eye and those people that don't are, perhaps unfairly, labelled as sheepish, shy or unconfident. So simply looking people in the eye implies the confidence needed to do it and not doing it implies a lack of confidence.

Also, when you are chatting to somebody and they don't give you the level of eye contact that you would perhaps expect, your brain then starts to wonder why they are doing this. Are they distracted, not interested in you or more interested in someone else or perhaps trying to hide something? This also therefore works against them creating a positive, confident impression.

On the flip side, if somebody gives you too much eye contact, how does that make you feel?

I'm guessing that the first word that popped into your head was "uncomfortable".

Again, your brain starts wondering why they are doing this? Are they being aggressive, avoiding looking at someone else or have you just got spinach stuck in your teeth!

Whatever their reason, it again has a negative impact on how they come across.

So the key word here is *appropriate* – enough to engage with them but not so much as to make them feel uncomfortable.

And it goes without saying that if you are talking to multiple people, they all need appropriate levels of eye contact!

*In the **RAIL** Framework I talked about defining your reasons for going to a networking event and that might involve identifying specific people with whom you would like to talk. It's possible for many reasons that the person with whom you are talking is not them. Perhaps your target is currently engaged with another group. Clearly you might be keeping an eye out in case that person becomes free but don't let that distract you from maintaining appropriate eye contact with whomever it is you are currently talking. You don't want people getting the feeling that you'd rather be talking to somebody else!*

PROWE**S**S

The first S in the **PROWESS** Framework stands for this: **Maintain a confident Stance**.

A strong, upright stance simply exudes confidence. Think of the professions that you see standing with this upright position. People in the armed forces, the police, politicians, royalty. Anybody whose job it is to exude an air of confidence will have this upright stance because it is a very confident way to stand. So if you're standing up straight, people think that you're confident.

So let's investigate what a good stance is.

It's time for an activity!

To help you to do this activity I have created a video that illustrates what needs to be done (and matches the textual description below). You can access that video in the Resources section of my website: www.intercog.co.uk.

What I need you to do is to find a door and then close it. Stand close to the door with your back towards it. Position your feet about a shoulder's width apart. Keeping that separation, put your heels against the bottom of the door. Now put your buttocks against the door and rest your shoulder blades against the door. Let your arms drape naturally by your sides. Finally, hold your head nice and relaxed on top of your neck and shoulders.

How does it feel? Unnatural? Awkward?

It wouldn't be surprising if it did!

Admittedly, this is a slightly exaggerated position because you're standing with your back actually touching the door. So the next thing to do is to take half a pace forward. Now *imagine* that you have the door at your back. Put your feet a shoulder's width apart. Align your heels, buttocks and shoulder blades against your imaginary door. Drape your arms and relax your head.

How does it feel now?

Probably less unnatural or awkward and yet you are standing in exactly the same way! It was most likely the door that was making it feel more peculiar or odd.

And talking of odd, your arms might feel a bit strange just hanging by your sides but there's a reason why they are there like that which I'll be back to in a moment.

So the goal, therefore, is that whenever you are networking, a good stance is a great way to exude confidence. This is especially true given that for a lot of the time at most networking events you'll be standing up.

For those parts of a networking event where you are seated, the principles still basically apply. Firstly, ensure your feet are flat on the floor and that you are sitting squarely on the chair. Then apply everything above from the buttocks up!

It's also important that you have good posture as you enter the room, so you metaphorically hit the ground running and enter the room looking already confident.

So I've got another activity for you!

To help you to do this activity I have created a video that illustrates what needs to be done (and matches the textual description below). You can access that video in the Resources section of my website: www.intercog.co.uk.

Open the door that you used in the last activity and stand underneath its frame, i.e. halfway through the door. Adopt your good stance as before.

Imagine that there is a piece of string hanging from the door frame and on the end of which there is a tennis ball. The length of the string is such that the tennis ball just rests ever so gently on top of your head.

Take a few paces away from the door, turn around and visualise the string and the tennis ball hanging from the frame. The goal here is to get the tennis ball to glance off the top of your head as you walk through the door. Of course, the only way you will be able to do this is if you have adopted your good stance by the time you get to the door frame. (Jumping up and heading the ball football-style is not really an option!)

So as you approach the door frame you need to go through those mental steps of your heels and your buttocks and your shoulder blades straightening up nicely with your head being nicely relaxed on your shoulders so that by the time you get to the door frame you've got your great stance and the tennis ball glances off your head.

I've used this activity on many occasions on training courses over the years and there are a few observations I'd like to share with you.

The first one is that people are sometimes so focused on straightening up and glancing the tennis ball off the top of their head that they forget to swing their arms whilst they are walking. That looks very peculiar and unnatural and is definitely not the impression we were going for! So let your arms do their natural thing and swing like they would normally do.

Secondly, for some reason people think they have to glance the ball off their nose. Don't ask me why they think this! They look even more odd than those with non-swinging arms. So keep your head nice and relaxed and let the tennis ball glance off the top of it.

And finally, almost everybody who does this activity on the course walks in with a big smile on their face. More on that in a moment...

If you adopt this mental strategy as you walk towards a door then you will enter the room with your good stance in place and look confident from the very moment you enter the room.

And it's such an easy technique to practise. Just think for a moment about how many doors you walk through every day. I suspect that you will have got to at least twenty by the time you leave for work in the morning. If you consciously think about using this technique every time you walk through a door then in two or three days it will become a habit and you will naturally therefore enter every room in the future looking confident.

Let's now come back to your arms. I talked earlier about letting your arms just hang loosely and naturally by your sides. It doesn't feel very natural at all and if you were to start talking your hands and arms would probably be itching to do things.

By having your arms naturally by your sides what it will do is encourage them to then gesture and those gestures help you to explain your story and the audience to understand what it is you're saying. Having them by your sides allows them to then do this. If your hands were in your pockets, or your arms were folded or behind your back, then that is going to get in the way of them doing what they want to do.

The other thing to consider here is the non-verbal message that your hands and arms are communicating. People with their hands in their pockets are often perceived as being insecure, not confident or disinterested. Folded arms can be seen as defensive whilst arms behind the back as overconfidence and pride. None of these are what you want to convey to the people with whom you are talking, especially if that's not how you are actually feeling.

Clearly, though, some people are not naturally big gesticulators and that's perfectly fine! For them, starting with their arms by their sides allows their hands to move into a naturally comfortable position, probably gently clasped in front of them, from where they can then gesture if needed.

The key point is that, however much you gesture, the good postural starting position allows you to do what you would naturally do and so you appear to be yourself. And if you are coming across as yourself, then surely you can't be nervous, can you?

> *As well as potentially gesturing, the other thing you will often have to use your hands for at networking events is holding food and/or drink. I'll come back to the idiosyncrasies of that, though, in the **Thought for Food** Framework.*

PROWES**S**

The final part of the **PROWESS** Framework is a very simple thing and that is just to **Smile**. Not a manic, nervous smile but a normal, natural smile.

So, picture somebody with a nice natural smile on their face. What emotions could they potentially be feeling?

Take a moment to jot a few down in this space:

I suspect on your list you will have things like:

- relaxed
- confident
- prepared
- knowledgeable
- content
- happy
- ready

That's because these are the sorts of emotions that you would naturally associate with somebody who's got a big smile on their face.

Now let's look at it from the other side. That person with the natural smile on their face, what emotions are they probably not feeling? What is it unlikely that they are feeling if they have a smile on their face?

Again, take a moment to jot a few of those down here:

On your list, you've probably got things like:

- nervous
- anxious
- scared
- unprepared
- sad
- sick

Surely nobody with a natural smile on their face would be feeling any of them, would they?

And therein lies the secret!

When we see somebody smiling naturally we instinctively assume that those positive emotions apply, that they are happy, ready and knowledgeable. That they're confident. It doesn't compute within us that they could be feeling any of those negative emotions because if they were, they wouldn't be smiling. We just naturally assume that all of those positive emotions are being felt and none of the negative ones are.

That's what is so simple, and effective, about this technique.

But it gets better!

There are also physiological benefits to smiling. When you smile certain chemicals are released in your body which affect you by lowering your heart rate and blood pressure, helping you to feel more relaxed and working as an anti-depressant, i.e. a mood lifter.

In simple terms, smiling actually makes you feel better! And if you feel better on the inside, you'll look better on the outside which is, after all, all your audience can see, which links back to the Confidence Cycle I mentioned earlier.

So clearly it's a good idea to have a nice natural smile on your face but it's not always so easy, however, to bring a smile to your face when you need one.

When I ask people how they can conjure a smile when they need one, they normally say something along the lines of "Think happy thoughts!". Those thoughts could be people, places, memories or whatever – it's different from person to person.

The link here, though, is to the **Preparation** in the **CAPS** Framework. As part of your preparation, work out what your "happy thoughts" are and then you can call on them when you need to. At the time of the networking event you don't want to be trying to work out what your "happy thoughts" are (while you're actually possibly stressed and nervous). You want to be actually thinking about them and smiling!

The time to think about those "happy thoughts" is before you enter the room so as you then enter the room the smile is naturally across your face. Anyone who sees you walk in will therefore think that you are confident and not wary of attending the event at all.

Smiling is also infectious. If you look at somebody who is smiling what is your natural response? To smile back!

As you chat to people, your smiling will help them to smile and their smiling will help you to smile, with the internal chemicals helping you both along the way and helping both of you to be more relaxed and open to conversation.

And as a final thought on this, smiling is a great way of being welcoming to people who are looking to join your group, which links back to what I mentioned earlier.

So smile!

Recap

Putting it all together, here's a summary of the **PROWESS** Framework:

Remember your **P**urpose
Remember that you are **R**eady
Be **O**utgoing
Be **W**elcoming
Maintain appropriate **E**ye contact
Maintain a confident **S**tance
Smile

Online Considerations

Let's look at each step in turn.

Remember your Purpose

This all still applies to an online event.

Remember that you are Ready

This still applies.

The other perspective here is that you need to know how to use the technology that will be used for the online event. You don't need to know everything about it, just enough to ensure that it does not get in the way of your making a good impression and interacting with the others there.

And also, of course, take a moment to remember that you do know how to use it!

Be Outgoing

30%.

That's the quoted figure as to how much energy is lost "down a camera". So to be you, the real you, you will need to give more energy to an online networking event than you would to an in-person one. So in that respect you need to be more outgoing.

Also, as I mentioned in the online considerations for the **RAIL** Framework, you might have little or no control over who you get to meet at an online event. Now for those people who are more introverted in nature, they might quite like the fact that they don't have to be brave and outgoing and approach other people whereas the more outgoing types might find it more restrictive than they would like.

At events where you do have a degree of control over who you get to meet, then you still need to be outgoing in practice to ensure that you meet the people you want to. Given the artificial nature of the online environment and the fact the people are less practiced at approaching people online than in person, it will most probably feel more awkward and unnatural to do this. This means that there is even more need to be even more outgoing online to overcome the potential increased reticence to do it.

Be Welcoming

You need to be welcoming online too.

People could be equally nervous about joining an online group as they might be about joining a physical one and so whatever you can do to put them at ease will be a bonus for them at the time (and then potentially for you in the future).

Maintain appropriate Eye contact

For an online event, the only way that people can see you is through your camera so, simply put, you need to look at the camera!

However, simple though that may seem to do, in practice, it's not always that straightforward. In an online environment where you can see the faces of the others there, your eyes will be drawn to those faces. It's the natural thing to do as you will feel like you are looking at them.

The snag is that you are not. If you are looking at the faces on your screen, you are looking at your screen, not looking at your camera. If you are not looking at your camera, then it will look to the others as if you are looking at something else and not them. That will have a detrimental effect on them in exactly the same way as if you were physically in the room in front of them and were not looking at them then either.

There are a number of things that you can do to help you to look at the camera more.

Simple though it may seem, the first approach is just to get into the habit of looking at your camera and not the faces on your screen. It will feel odd to you because it will feel like you are not looking at the others there. However, to them, it will feel like you are looking at them.

Because you are not looking at those faces, you may miss out on some visual clues from them but the more that you practise looking at the camera, the more that you will learn to pick up those clues with your peripheral vision. This is, in effect, what happens in reality when you are in the same room anyway.

The second approach is to move the faces on the screen as close to your camera as possible to reduce the feeling of distance between where you need to be looking and your audience looking back. For laptops, iPads etc, this normally means moving the windows to be just below your camera.

Another alternative is to buy a separate camera and use that. Often this extra camera is placed on top of the monitor/screen and so again it's a case of moving the windows on the screen to be just below that camera. It could also be positioned on a tripod in front of your screen so that the faces are behind it. It would almost feel then as if you were looking through your camera to the other attendees, although the camera will obscure their faces slightly.

Whichever approach you take, however, as with most things to do with networking, and technology in particular, practice makes better!

When I was talking about online considerations in the **RAIL** Framework, I mentioned potentially having extra information on or around your screen, a second screen or on your desk. Whilst this is a valid approach, the obvious is worth stating that when you are looking at the extra information you are not looking at your camera and therefore not looking at the others there, which is not ideal. The only exception to this is if you can cunningly position that extra information so that it is behind your camera so you are effectively looking at both at the same time.

Maintain a confident Stance

If you want to stand up whilst attending an online event (as you would at an in-person one) then feel free to do so! If you do, everything above about a confident stance still applies. The main thing that you need to ensure is that the environment is set up accordingly, e.g. that the camera is at eye level, the sound is OK etc. In other words, all of those extra online considerations I mentioned for the **Logistics** part of the **RAIL** Framework.

Most people, however, sit down when attending an online networking event. In this case, the confident stance principles still hold, but need to be adapted:

- set the height of your chair to be such that your shins are vertical, your feet are flat on the floor and your thighs are horizontal
- your buttocks should be at the rear of the seat with your back going straight up the back of the chair
- your arms should naturally come down so your hands are in your lap
- your head needs to be resting in a relaxed way on your shoulders
- and also:
  - avoid leaning on arm rests
  - avoid rocking backwards and forwards excessively
  - try not to spin around too much

In the same way that there is some movement when you chat standing up, there should be some movement when you chat sitting down as well.

And as I have mentioned before, regardless of whether you are standing or sitting, ensure that your camera is at eye level. If it's too low, the other attendees will be looking up your nose and it will also increase the number of chins that you appear to have – neither of these are desirable! If it's too high, you will look aloof and get a bad neck as well. You need to be resting your head in a relaxed and even way whilst looking directly into the camera.

Smile

You still need to smile!

The SHINE Framework

For helping you to make a glowing first impression.

Here's a transcript of two people meeting each other for the first time at a networking event:

Hi, I'm Jane Smith.

Nice to meet you Jane! I'm John.

Nice to meet you too John!

What else would be happening as they say these words?

I'm guessing that you would probably be imagining that they would be shaking hands whilst looking each other in the eye. To get off to a friendly start, they may well even be smiling.

And that's really all there is to it!

Everything you need to make a great first impression is right there above:
- **S**mile
    - it's a welcoming thing to do
    - it starts things off in a friendly tone
    - if you smile, they are likely to smile back
    - when anyone smiles it physically makes that person feel better
- **H**andshake
    - the pretty universal greeting gesture – in fact, it's probably rude not to!
    - make sure your handshake is appropriate:
        - not a wet fish
        - not a bone cruncher
        - only use one hand
            - some people put a second hand on the other's hand, forearm, elbow or shoulder but I personally find that a bit odd and uncomfortable
    - gauge the duration of the shake from the other person
        - you'll normally get a feel for how long they want to shake your hand
- **I**ntroductions
    - they can be short and sweet
    - don't just say "Hello"

- <u>N</u>ames
  - repeat their name:
    - it shows you are taking an interest in them – "be interested", people like that
    - it also helps you to remember their name
  - don't forget to reciprocate and say your name too
    - whether or not you choose to say your surname as well is up to you - John chose not to in the above example
- <u>E</u>ye contact
  - make sure it's appropriate:
    - not too long
    - not too brief

The goal of this **SHINE** Framework is therefore to help you to remember the five constituent parts that are needed to make a good first impression. I appreciate that this is not rocket science but it's important that all five are done. Consider for a moment the impression that someone would make on you in this scenario if:

- they didn't smile
- they crushed your hand for five seconds whilst shaking it
- they didn't even say hello
- they didn't say their own name
- they weren't interested enough in you to repeat your name
- they gave you only a fleeting glance before looking around the room

So even though it's simple, it's very much worth following. You can only ever make a first impression once so make sure it's a good one!

You'll no doubt notice some of the themes from earlier parts of the book in the above: smiling, being welcoming, taking an interest in the other person and maintaining appropriate eye contact.

There is also one other reason why this framework really shines (last intended pun) and that links back to what I was saying about confidence earlier in this book. Many people don't like shaking hands. In fact, many people are really nervous about doing it. Add into the mix the potentially stressful nature of the networking event itself and you may well therefore be approached by a sheepish person with a quivering, sweaty palm that's coming your way!

And that's where the **SHINE** Framework really helps. Remembering these five simple elements for making a great first impression will help them to look less nervous and more confident. And if they *look* confident...

*I have created a video that shows the **SHINE** Framework in action and demonstrates the points mentioned above. You can access that video in the Resources section of my website: www.intercog.co.uk.*

Recap

Putting it all together, here's a summary of the **SHINE** Framework:

Smile
Give an appropriate **H**andshake
Exchange pleasant **I**ntroductions
Use reciprocal **N**ames
Maintain appropriate **E**ye contact

Online Considerations

When meeting somebody online it's a bit tricky to actually shake hands!

However, for all of the reasons above, it's still good practice to:

- **S**mile
- exchange pleasant **I**ntroductions
- use reciprocal **N**ames
- maintain appropriate **E**ye contact

So SHINE becomes SINE and the mathematician (or nerd) in me finds that ironic and intriguing!

Why?

Because the word that would most normally follow the word SINE in a conversation would be the word wave (as in Sine Wave) and what do people now tend to do when saying "hello" and "goodbye" at an online event because they can't shake hands? They wave!

Thought for Food

For keeping you out of "sticky" situations whilst you're networking.

Shaking hands with cold hands, hot hands or sticky hands is never a great way to make a first impression!

It can be a bit daunting and worrying for people at a networking event with the prospect of coordinating all of that eating, drinking, talking and handshaking. Fortunately, there are some simple tips which you can follow to help with this:

- never have both hands full at the same time
  - that will leave one free for shaking hands
- make use of nearby tables
  - this will save you having to hold things
- drink with your left hand
  - (unless you have a valid reason not to)
  - if you have a cold or hot drink in your right hand when somebody approaches you, you will naturally transfer it to your left hand (or put it down) but your hand will still have some residual temperature left over from your drink which will then be unpleasant or unexpected when you shake hands
    - this will not make a great impression
  - if you drink with your left hand that will leave your right hand at room temperature and won't lead to any unpleasant surprises for the other person
- hold your plate in your right hand and eat with your left hand
  - (unless you have a valid reason not to)
  - if you are eating with your right hand then it will accumulate over time residual food which you are then going to smear onto the other person's hand when you shake it
    - that's unpleasant and unimpressive!
  - if you hold your plate in your right hand and eat with your left hand as someone approaches you, you can transfer the plate to your left hand (or put it down) and then your right hand will be free and at room temperature, or thereabouts
- have access to a napkin
  - you never know when you might need one

I have created a video on how to cope with refreshments that goes into more detail with examples of how to do it in practice. You can access that video in the Resources section of my website: www.intercog.co.uk.

Oh, and of course, don't talk with your mouth full!

One way to avoid a lot of the above, however, is to eat either before you go or after you return from the event. This may not be possible but is an option worth considering.

Online Considerations

Clearly, if you are not attending an in-person event, most of the above does not apply.

However, for an online event, you are in control of the environment around you and therefore the food and drink that you consume during that event. Other than having a drink handy, it's probably wise to not have any other refreshments around. Don't be tempted to eat just because you can because you've got food in the house!

The HELPful Introduction

For helping you to introduce contacts to each other and for them to introduce new people to you.

Picture the scene.

You're at a networking event having a great conversation with a new contact or maybe somebody you've known for a while. It doesn't really matter which. Let's call him George.

You're listening intently being very interested in what George is saying, using your wonderful questioning techniques to draw out information and guide the conversation along the lines that you would like it to go.

As you're chatting, however, George mentions a problem that he's got and, as you hear more, you realise that you know somebody who solves that sort of problem. You know somebody who could help George. Let's call them Paula.

So what are you going to do?

Of course, you're going to offer to introduce George to Paula.

All you need to do is say, "Would you like me to introduce you to somebody who could help you with that?". It's such a simple question and it's also such a powerful question.

It's highly unlikely that George is going to say no, to effectively say, "Yes I have a problem but no I don't want any help to solve it." The problem is clearly causing George some issues or else he wouldn't have brought it up in the conversation in the first place.

Very few people in that situation would refuse the offer of help. "Yes, that would be great. Thank you!", they would normally reply.

So you introduce George to Paula with the best of intentions that George's problem will be solved.

And if it is, how are you going to look?

George is going to think that you're great because his problem has been solved.

Paula is going to be grateful to you because of the work you have passed her way.

That's a lot of brownie points!

So what will happen at some point in the future? George and Paula will no doubt return the favour and make an introduction for you. It's the Law of Reciprocity!

When you make an introduction, always provide some context with that introduction. So in the above case, provide some context to Paula about why you would like to introduce George to her. It's also worthwhile letting Paula know what your relationship is with George, how well you know him etc. As the introducer, your reputation and relationships are on the line and so expectations need to be set correctly.

But if we stop for a moment and examine what needed to be in place for such a simple, but powerful, introduction to be made, you can only really make this sort of helpful introduction if you understand how your contact Paula helps other people.

So once again, understanding what people do in terms of how they help other people is crucial to allow you to do this, to make those introductions.

Let's now turn it around the other way.

Let's imagine that one of your contacts, Trevor, is chatting to somebody who you don't even know. Let's call them Alice. Trevor is listening intently (of course) and at some point in the conversation Alice says something that catches Trevor's attention. It's something that you could help her with.

Of course, what you would like Trevor to do at that point is to say, "Would you like me to introduce you to somebody who could help you with that?". In this case, that somebody is you!

But again, Trevor can only really make that simple offer of an introduction if he understands how you help other people and that links back to what I covered in the **ICE** Framework.

And as a final comment on this, I'd like you to stop and think for a moment.

Using the example from above, what is it that Alice might say to Trevor that would make Trevor then think of you? Consider that question for all of the different ways in which you help people.

As you network with your contacts, you can therefore be proactively planting seeds in the minds of your contacts along those lines, so when those statements do crop up, the light bulb will go off in your contacts' minds and the connections can potentially be made with a **HELPful** introduction.

Online Considerations
This is equally useful and important for online networking too.

Think HRH

For helping you to have a productive and confident mindset when networking.

The acronym HRH is normally used for His/Her Royal Highness when referring to people such as Queen Elizabeth or Prince Charles. I'm not for a moment suggesting that you impersonate royalty when networking though!

Having said that, there is no doubt that the Royal Family do meet a lot of people every year and, while this is not strictly networking as such, the Royal Family are certainly adept at the art of meeting other people and have a perceived high level of confidence when they do it. They are also certainly world-class hosts.

So perhaps, the comparison with royalty on the confidence side of things and networking is actually not a bad one…

In reality, though, in this framework, HRH stands for something else. It's a mindset-based approach of three things to think about whilst you are networking, three things to keep at the forefront of your thoughts:

> Think **H**ost(ess)
> Think **R**elationship
> Think **H**elper

The first aspect brings in a new angle as to how you can have a confident mindset whilst networking. The final two aspects are, in many ways, summaries of other things that have been mentioned in the book so far and are a nice way to draw this part of the book to a close.

Let's look at each letter in turn.

Think **H**ost(ess)

Now I'm not suggesting that you try to take over an event here. That would simply be rude and highly counterproductive! This is more about taking on a similar mindset to what a host(ess) might do.

A good host(ess) feels at home at an event, is comfortable talking to any guest and can easily make introductions between guests. They can easily join and leave conversations and would never leave anyone standing on their own. Everyone treats them as if they belong at that event. It's a beneficial positive mindset to have whilst at an event without actually taking it over.

Along similar lines, here are a few other things you can try:
- offer to help with the event in some capacity, e.g.:
  - help with giving out the badges and collateral at the start of the event:
    - everyone has to talk to you and will do so quite openly and naturally
    - it is therefore much easier to then approach them later for another chat
    - you could also "pre-book" your chat with your target(s) by asking when you give them their badge if you could grab a few minutes with them later
  - help with the refreshments:
    - if people need to come to you to get their refreshments it's so easy to chat to them whilst doing so and you can then more easily loop with them later at the event for having done so

I have a friend who has an annual summer BBQ. He always asks me to do the cooking and I always say yes. Why? Because everyone has to come to see me to get their food and so I get to meet everyone at the party and it's so easy to start up a conversation. It's the most social place to be! It might not be a networking event per se but the principle still holds (and it's still a great way to practise my networking skills).

- it might be that you're taking the food to them (on platters etc)
  - you get implicit permission to approach them
  - offering them your refreshments is a natural ice breaker
  - you can briefly chat to them at that point
  - you can then more easily loop with them later at the event for having done so

I have been to parties in the past where I was asked to bring the "nibbles" for the event. I duly arrived, put the nibbles out on a tray and proceeded to wander around offering the nibbles to all of the guests, some of whom I knew and some I didn't. As I introduced myself as the requested provider of the nibbles, no-one thought it odd that I was walking round with them and yet I could easily connect with everyone there. The principle and opportunity to practise still hold here too.

- if you can't be involved officially, "loiter" near the food:
  - as people approach the food you could casually say, "Have you tried the <insert your favourite buffet food item here> – they're really tasty!"
  - it's a very simple and unimposing way to start up a conversation
  - it's also quite natural to continue that conversation as you then both wander away from the food table

- simply offer to get someone a drink
    - you're showing an interest in them, which will make you appear interesting to them
    - it's a kind and positive thing to do
    - when you return with the drink you have implicit permission to chat to the person to whom you are giving the drink

Clearly, the above are situation specific but they, and variations on their themes, do work in helping you to meet other people at an event.

Remember though, respect the actual host(ess) and don't do anything that's more akin to stalking…

Think Relationship

Here's that misquote from Kevin Costner again:

> If you build the relationships, business will come!

Thinking back to when I was talking about **Joining the Dots**, it will take patience, practice and purpose to build those relationships, i.e. to get more, bigger dots.

And people ultimately buy from people and then only from people they know, like and trust. That means that the focus needs to be on the building of the relationships.

As I said back in the **"Don't Sell, Build!"** core principle, it's not about selling at all…

Think Helper

This is the 107th time that "help" has appeared in this book so far. (yes – I have actually counted them)

It's no accident that the number is so high as having a mindset based on understanding how people help other people is vital for successful, productive networking.

It's important to:
- find out how the people that you are talking to can help other people
    - this also includes how they could help you too
- have a plan as to how you can find this out
    - "Be interested"
- ensure that the other people there understand how you help other people
    - this also includes specifically how you could help the people you are talking to at that moment

- have a plan as to how you can help people to understand this
  - "Be interesting"
  - know how to break the ICE in an interesting and memorable way
  - consider what people might say that would get other people to think of you and how to plant those thoughts in your conversations with those people

Taking this approach then allows you to make **HELPful Introduction**s so that you can help people to help other people (and so that in the future they will therefore probably help you too).

Recap
Putting it all together, here's a summary of the **HRH** Framework:

> Think **H**ost(ess)
> Think **R**elationship
> Think **H**elper

Online Considerations
Having a **Host(ess)** mindset works equally well online as it does in person.

There is also the potential to offer to help with an event as some technologies have the ability for there to be "co-hosts" at an online event. Co-hosts help with some of the logistical and management elements of the execution of the event so that the actual host can focus on the attendees. Co-hosts therefore have the implicit permission to interact more directly with the other attendees and that will facilitate some aspects of your networking were you able to be one.

NOTE: I use the term "host" and "co-host" here as those are the technical terms used by most software solutions.

Clearly, though, the "help with the food and drink" perspective is not really applicable for an online event.

The **Relationship** and **Helper** aspects of **Think HRH** are as equally applicable to online networking as they are to in-person events.

The additional aspect about which you can help people is the technology. Many people who network online are not that familiar with the technology being used and this will potentially get in the way of their networking activities.

If you are knowledgeable in the technology being used you can help others to use that technology more effectively with polite suggestions and useful nudges along the way. Not only will this help them to get more out of their online networking, it will also make a positive impression on them which will stand you in good stead for the future.

Part 4

Networking on Social Media

Before I get to networking via Social Media, don't forget that all of the things in the first part of this book, the Foundations of Networking, also apply to your networking activities on Social Media as well, i.e.:

- *effective networking is purposefully interacting with others*
- *don't sell, build relationships*
- *building a network takes patience, practice and purpose*
- *confidence is the sum total of your audience-focus, preparation and skills*

LinkedIn, Facebook, Twitter, WhatsApp, Instagram, TikTok, YouTube to name but a few.

The list just goes on and on, it seems to get bigger every day and people's favourites and what's considered to be the "best" platform seems to change almost weekly. You could easily spend all day just trying to keep up with what's out there!

So the good news is that, for the purposes of this part of the book, I'm not going to be specifically talking about any platforms in detail.

And why is that good news you might ask?

Well, it's good news because however much the technological alternatives change, whatever becomes "flavour of the month" or "old fashioned", the content in this part of the book will still apply. So if you want to change the platform you use, you can, you just have to work out how to do what you need to be doing using that new technology. No doubt there will always be videos on YouTube (or its future equivalent) to help you to do that too!

So what's in this part of the book then?

Principles, similarities and differences.

There are many principles for effective networking at events that can be directly applied to networking conducted via Social Media so, in this part of the book, I'll reflect on those principles that I covered in Parts 2 and 3 that apply to Social Media as well.

In doing so, there will be some similarities in the way that they are relevant as well as some differences in what you can do and how you can do it. There are also some things that you can do via Social Media that can't be done at events, even online ones.

So let's start off with the first basic principle: whenever you post on Facebook, send out a Tweet or post a new video on TikTok, for example, you are networking. It might not feel like networking but it is because you are interacting with someone (as per my definition at the start of the book). Intrinsically therefore, any time you are doing something via Social Media you are networking.

So what, with whom, where, why, when and how much should/could you be doing?

These are the questions I will be answering in this part of the book by considering:

- to what level you can take your activities
- how you can work out who and where your audience is
- what your purpose is for using Social Media
- how to spend your time effectively
- how to create an interesting and social online persona

I'll cover each of these aspects in turn in the following sections.

> *Remember - I have structured this book to allow me to focus on events and Social Media separately. They are, however, not mutually exclusive. In fact, to be better at networking as a whole, I would suggest that you need to be attending meetings **and** using Social Media. What percentage of your time is spent doing which is, of course, up to you!*

The A to D of Social Media Involvement

For considering the level to which you want to go with Social Media.

How much time, effort and money do you want to invest in your Social Media networking activities?

There are so many things to consider, so many alternatives about what and how much could be done that it's not always easy to work out what "level" to go to.

What I've done, therefore, is to distil the multitude of options and approaches into a 4-level model, the **A to D of Social Media Involvement**.

The model looks like this:

Level of Involvement	Description
Dynamic	A fully engaged presence making the most of the platform's capabilities.
Contributory	An active presence with proactive contributions and bi-directional interaction with others.
Basic	An up-to-date passive presence for information only with minimal reactive-only interaction.
Absent	No presence.

The higher the level, the more time, effort and possibly money is involved as is the higher the potential for getting more rewards, although I use the word *potential* deliberately as things still need to be done effectively.

The other consideration here is that the level of your involvement can vary by platform as you might do more on one platform and less on another. The model essentially, therefore, could be turned into a grid where you determine to which level you will go for each platform. For example:

Level	Website	LinkedIn	Facebook	Twitter	YouTube	etc
Dynamic		X				
Contributory			X			
Basic	X				X	
Absent				X		

You'll notice that I've got a column for your website because, if you have one, I see it as being part of your online presence and so falls under the title of "Social Media" and therefore needs to be considered here.

So let's have a brief look at each of the levels in turn before coming back to the consideration of which level to choose.

Level A – Absent

This level is easy – you are not doing anything on that platform.

You have no presence at all. In effect, you are ignoring it and any potential networking opportunities that might come via this channel.

Level B – Basic

At the basic level, you have a presence on a platform, but it is essentially a passive presence.

You have information that you present that is up to date and informative and, hopefully, interesting to the people that are viewing it

The information provides details on what you do and how you help people. That information also includes contact information in case people would like to get in touch and connect with you.

You update that information as required to keep it up to date, for example, as new products come in and so on, but really it is a passive presence which is there for reference for other people who are on Social Media.

Yes, you might well review and accept (or reject) connection requests from other people but that's kind of all you do as you don't proactively go out looking for other connections. If somebody comes looking for you, they can find you and your information but that's about it.

In summary:

Level	Description
Basic	The platform has information about what you do. That information describes how you help people. The platform has contact details. Information is kept up to date. Connection requests are reviewed and accepted/rejected.

Level C – Contributory

This level builds on the previous level.

This is where you start to be more proactive with your networking activities. You start to proactively send out connection requests and start to build your network, rather than just letting people come to you (which hopefully will also happen of course).

When you send out invitations and reply to connection requests you personalise them and make them more social. You will probably also follow up with new connections afterwards as a separate and additional action.

Where the platform allows, you keep an eye on who has viewed your profile/information and take action accordingly.

This is the level where you start to create and post content on a regular basis, content that is tailored to the audience at which you are aiming. You may also start to share with your own audience content, articles and testimonials that other people have created.

And as people view and respond to your content and posts, you actively consider what you then do as a result of that, how you then respond yourself, which, of course, you might choose not to do as you won't (and indeed feasibly can't) respond to everything.

In summary:

Level	Description
Contributory	Proactive invitation requests are made. Invitations and acceptances are socialised. Accepted connection requests are followed up. Profile views are reviewed and actioned. Content is created and posted regularly. Content is tailored to audiences. Relevant content, articles and testimonials are shared. All audience responses are reviewed. Some audience responses are replied to.

Level D – Dynamic

This level builds on the previous two levels.

At this level you are starting to take advantage of the full range of techniques that can be used to share content on that platform. That content can be shaped dynamically for relevance and also repurposed for different platforms.

This is also the level where you create groups centred on a common theme and encourage audience engagement, responses and collaboration. The goal is to create a "sense of community" by having an active and supportive set of people within that group. Almost a "mini-network" you could say.

And the other thing that you would be doing is tracking and reviewing engagement and evaluating its effectiveness, reception and enjoyment – it is *Social* Media after all! These reflection-based activities will then allow you to shape future content and engagement.

In summary:

Level	Description
Dynamic	A range of techniques are used to share content. Content is shaped dynamically for relevance. Content is repurposed for different platforms. Groups/communities are formed on a common theme. Audience engagement and responses are encouraged. Engagement is tracked and reviewed. Previous enjoyment informs on future content.

So which level do you go to?

As I mentioned before, that is up to you!

In essence it's like having a jar which represents the amount of time, effort and money that you can allocate to your networking activities as a whole. You need to decide how you fill that jar and therefore need to consider:

- Will you be doing events or Social Media or both?
- On which Social Media platform(s) will you be present?
- To which level will you be going for each platform?

So, weigh up the considerations, create a plan and go for it!

In my experience, everybody's plan is different. I know people who only do events and don't do Social Media at all, and people who only do social media and don't attend any events. And I know plenty of people who are somewhere in the middle too! Any of these approaches can work, if they are the correct thing to do.

And then, after a period of time, review how it is going and, if necessary, come up with a new plan!

It's exactly the same principle as I mentioned earlier in the book when I was talking about reviewing return on investment for events but now you are also considering your Social Media activities and are looking at your networking as a whole. It's a crucially important thing to do as your networking activities need to be effective and if they are not, you're wasting time, effort and money. You also have the implied opportunity costs of what you could be doing instead.

So if needs be, take some things out of your jar and replace them with different things. (and then rinse and repeat this process again and again over time)

Looking forward then to what's in the rest of this book, the following sections will help with your considerations and planning and therefore what to potentially put into your jar. However, although I won't explicitly map the upcoming content specifically to the different levels of involvement above, you will be able to see how it applies to them and where it might fit.

Define and Find your Audience

For working out who and where they are.

When you attend a networking event there is a finite sized audience there. On Social Media, your audience is bigger. A lot bigger!

In the same way that online networking events potentially remove geographical restrictions, Social Media does too. When you use Social Media as your vehicle for networking, the whole world is listening (potentially)...

That audience is also a lot more accessible and it is much easier to try and connect with them as that's what the technology is designed for.

However, simply spamming out connection requests is like standing in the corner of a networking event and just shouting at everyone. Yes, it's technically possible for that approach to work on the odd occasion but the more likely result is that you'll just annoy everyone and they will ignore you.

There's no way that you would do that at an event so why would you do it via Social Media?

So it still holds true that, for effective use of Social Media, you need to work out who your target audience is. In the **RAIL** Framework I talked about how you would go about this before an event and many of those principles still hold. There are some differences when using Social Media, however, differences that can, in many ways, be thought of as advantages.

For example, at an event, the delegate list is only an approximation of who will be at the event (no shows and late additions see to that). However, most Social Media platforms have a search capability, some of which are really sophisticated. They have, in effect, the "ultimate delegate list". Couple that with the fact that you are effectively talking about people's online presence, you can almost think of them as being in permanent attendance, although I appreciate that their actual presence is totally dependent on their activity levels (other people on Social Media might be operating at level B, C or D). They are therefore always approachable (if not responsive). You just need to work out who you would like to approach and how (which I'll come back to in a moment).

In the **RAIL** Framework I also suggested that you do some research on your target audience in preparation for the event. The same is true for your Social Media activities. Find out information about your audience *before* you connect with them as this will allow you to introduce yourself in a more personal/focused way.

*In the **HELPful Introduction** Framework I recommended providing some context when you were introducing people to each other. In the same way, when you are connecting with someone via Social Media, always provide some context as to why you are making that connection request (assuming the platform allows you to do that). If you have researched that person then this is much easier to do well.*

The next thing to work out is your plan for approaching them, the Social Media equivalent of walking up to somebody at a networking event and saying "Hello". Fortunately, most Social Media platforms allow you to go directly to your target audience and introduce yourself which simplifies this step in the process.

*That all being said, you still have to click/tap on the button and actually do it! Many people fear making connections online in the same way they do in person. I'll talk a bit more about this in the **Interesting and Sociable** section later.*

Of course, as is true for making connections at events, being introduced to somebody by somebody else is so much more powerful (and often less scary) than introducing yourself. So if you can engineer/arrange for that to happen then do so. Think about who you know who knows your target audience and ask them to introduce you.

And this is again where Social Media has an advantage. Many platforms allow you to see those people who your connections already know, e.g. LinkedIn connections, Facebook friends, Twitter followers etc. You can use that information to your advantage in requesting introductions to be made.

There's nothing stopping you using this sort of information from Social Media channels to orchestrate introductions at networking events as well. It's all part of your research and planning.

The final thing to consider is *where* your target audience might be. In the **RAIL** Framework I talked about the fact that there were different sorts of networking events that you can attend and that thinking about the sorts of people that would go to those different types of events would help you to choose which events to attend to get the best potential access to your target audience. A similar principle holds for Social Media.

Not everyone is present on all Social Media platforms. Some people prefer LinkedIn, others Facebook, others Instagram and so on. If you want to connect with your target audience, then you need to know which platforms your target audiences use so you can approach them on that platform. This requires research, in the same way as working out which events you think they might attend.

 *The Target Audience Preparation Worksheet that I mentioned earlier when talking about events is equally applicable and useful for your Social Media planning as well. You can download that document from the Resources section on my website: www.intercog.co.uk.*

Have Clear Aims

For defining your online purpose.

LinkedIn folklore talks about the magical "500+ connections" figure. Once you have more than 500 connections, LinkedIn stops reporting the actual number of connections that you have and just says "500+" because you have *so many*. You've made it, you're seriously connected, your network is huge!

But is it just full of very small dots? Do you actually have any decently sized dots in there? It may be huge but is it any good?

Perhaps not so much these days, but certainly in the early days, there was a tendency for people to be driven to get as many connections as possible in their networks. It was almost a "status symbol" thing.

I have to be honest and admit that I fell into this trap too. If I look at my LinkedIn connections now there are people on there that I can't remember and struggle to work out where I knew them from in the first place! It's sad but true...

Whilst having a good number of connections in a network can be beneficial, it's not the number per se that you should be aiming for. It's the quality of the relationships. In other words, larger dots, not necessarily more dots.

In the **RAIL** Framework the **R** stood for "What is your **Reason** for going networking?". I encouraged you to think carefully about what you wanted to achieve at each and every networking event that you went to. Was it to:

- meet new people
- catch up with existing contacts
- arrange follow on meetings
- etc

I also suggested that you quantify your goals as much as you could and that included taking into account the people that you wanted to meet (the **A** in the framework stood for **Audience**). In this way you could then evaluate the effectiveness of your networking more precisely.

This all applies to your networking via Social Media as well. In the same way that you had clear goals and aims for your networking at events you need them for your Social Media activities too.

Some of those aims might be very similar on Social Media. There will also be some differences.

Let's go back to the examples above:

- to make some new *online* contacts
    - you can identify those targets in the same way as for events, e.g.:
        - people you know versus people you don't know
            - you might know them in the real world but have not yet connected via Social Media
        - named individuals, e.g. John Smith from ABC Industries
        - specific companies
        - industries/business sectors
        - roles within a business
        - levels within a business
        - size of business (employees, turnover etc)
        - etc
        - (these could be combined)
    - you can then work out how you are going to approach them, e.g. directly or via a shared connection
- to catch up with existing *online* contacts
    - at a networking event, "catch up with" basically meant "have a chat with", however, in the world of Social Media, "catch up with" could mean:
        - emailing/messaging them directly
        - having an online chat
        - having a video meeting
        - and stretching this slightly, creating some content on a channel that your audience can read at a later date
            - this is perhaps a "one-directional" catching up approach, unless of course they comment on/reply to that content
- arrange a follow on meeting
    - this might also be online as there are many technologies that provide this capability
    - however, it might also be in person as for some people, their primary aim is to use Social Media as the vehicle to get to the point where they can have an in-person relationship with their target audience

Regardless of the reasons above, though, there are some key differences in the way goals need to be set for online activities and these relate to the SMARTness of those aims.

Firstly, what are you **M**easuring?

I alluded to this at the start of this section. Is it the number of connections that you really should be measuring or the amount of interaction that you have with those connections? Are you counting the number of dots in your network or measuring the size of those dots? And what quantitative measures can you use to measure the "size" of your dots?

If you post some content, do you measure, for example, the number of views, the number of likes or the number of comments? What is your aim? For people to see it or for people to react to it?

Just "pumping out" lots of content and measuring that to say that you're very active is not a valid metric. It's exactly the same principle as shouting at a networking event and something you don't want to be doing.

And are you bothered about who? Do you want to set goals for specific people, or types of people or types of businesses?

There are lots of things to consider when you think about how you are going to measure the effectiveness of your Social Media activities.

The other big difference is to do with **T**ime. When you go to a networking event it has a defined time associated with it. You therefore set your goals for that event and implicitly, therefore, the time you allocate to being at that event.

There are no equivalent natural timing constraints for Social Media. So when you are setting your goals, you will need to apply some "artificial" timings to those goals which then links to what it will be **R**ealistic to **A**chieve. For example:

- 100 views within a month
- 10 likes within a week
- 2 replies within a day

The timeframes you assign will depend on the nature of the content. For example, something that is very topical, and perhaps therefore short-lived with regard to its relevance, would naturally have a shorter timeframe associated with it compared to content that is more generic.

Be Effective, not Busy

For making the most out of your time on Social Media.

If there is one environment in which it's easy to be a "busy fool" it's Social Media!

"Oh, I'll just read these posts and see what John has said and then I'll have a look at that link and catch the latest videos before I scroll down pages of potential connections to see who I could connect with and then, oh look, some more posts to read…"

In the same way that it's not effective to go to every possible networking event, it's not effective to do everything on every platform on Social Media. Choices need to be made and those choices need to be made according to the aims that you have for your online networking activities and where you will find your target audiences.

So it's OK to not be everywhere, all of the time.

As I suggested right back at the start of the book, *effective* networking is *purposeful* interaction with other people. This applies to your Social Media activities as well and questions that need to be addressed here are:

- How much time are you going to spend on your activities and when are you going to do them?
- Where are you going to spend your efforts?
- How are you going to reuse your content?
- Who is going to do it?
- What is your plan?

How much time are you going to spend on your activities and when are you going to do them?

You only have a certain amount of time you can spend on your Social Media networking activities so that time needs to be spent wisely. There are a number of aspects to this and the first step is work out how much time you are going to spend doing it and when you are going to do it.

Because Social Media is so readily accessible, it's easy to do a bit here, do a bit there and end up getting distracted. It very much lends itself to a "dabbling here and there" approach. However, if you compare that to a networking event, it's very different. An event takes up a defined chunk of time, time during which you are dedicated and focused on the act of networking. (There may be some time required before and after it for travel, preparation, following up etc.) In some ways you could think of it as "quality networking time".

You could take the same approach with your Social Media activities by blocking out times of days in your diary for your Social Media networking activities.

During that time, focus solely on those activities and don't get distracted by other things. Whilst it's nice to get an instant response to a post or video etc, most people recognise that there is normally a delay in people replying and so it's OK to not reply instantly. Clearly, you should reply in a timely and polite manner to those things that you need/want to reply to but it doesn't have to be instantly. How much time you allocate and when you allocate it will depend on the level to which you are taking your networking activities but taking this approach can work very well, not only in terms of your own effectiveness but also for setting the expectations of your audience as to the frequency and rapidity of your responses.

The key here is to interact often enough to make your online presence appear to be dynamic and reactive but to not spend so much time focussing on it that it impacts on other things that you need to do.

This approach is also beneficial because people like consistency and predictability. If you habitually reply every day first thing in the morning, then people will get used to that. If you are actively generating content on Social Media, for example, at the same time each week, then your audience will come to expect something from you at that time. It almost becomes part of their activities too. People will therefore potentially start looking forward to your contributions because they know they are coming.

It would be great to be in the situation where your audience are waiting with bated breath for your next contribution in the same way that they might do for the next episode of their favourite TV show: "New episodes coming weekly!"

In many ways, this is the same as in the world of networking events where you will often find that the same people attend the same sorts of events on a regular basis. If you are going to one of those events you can almost expect them to be there. This consistency, or predictability, can be very helpful when planning your networking activities.

Where are you going to spend your efforts?

When I was talking about attending events, I suggested working out which networking events provide the most return on investment and then attending those more than others. It's exactly the same principle with Social Media and as I mentioned earlier in the **Audience** section, it similarly pays to investigate which Social Media channels/platforms your target audience(s) frequent and to prioritise activities in those channels/platforms.

Some channels/platforms offer "sub-channels", for example, groups. For the purposes of this discussion, however, I'm not going to differentiate to that level as they are really just somewhere else you might find your audience and therefore

> might need to spend some of your time and efforts. Admittedly groups might be a bit more focused and therefore smaller in size perhaps...

You can also gauge which channels work well for you by examining the interactions that you get with your audience. Some interactions, like replies, likes or views for example are perhaps the most obvious to look at. Some platforms provide you with more information such as seeing who has viewed your page, visited your profile or how many times you have appeared in searches. All of this information will give you a good idea of where to focus as it can give you an indication of the interest level that people have in you and your content. In many ways, you can potentially find out more about how much people are interested in you via Social Media than you might be able to ascertain at a networking event.

And then there is the consideration of who is viewing/interacting with you, what their characteristics are and what "potential" they might have. It sounds a little harsh but you will probably have to pick and choose who to follow up with as you won't have time to interact with everyone. It's the same premise as not being able to talk to everyone at an event.

> Just as with events though, don't forget that you don't know who someone you don't know might know and so "potential" might not be instantly obvious...

This might also vary across platforms and for different parts of your business. For example, one of my contacts, Charlie, knows that:

- her business clients come from LinkedIn so that's where she posts topical, informative posts with a dash of personality to encourage discussion
- her one-to-one coaching clients prefer Facebook and Instagram and so on those platforms she focuses on bite-sized content delivered in fun ways that show her passion and personality and are likely to be watched and shared

> Charlie comes across as both interesting and sociable with her Social Media activities. Her online persona is therefore very much in line with her real-life personality. I'll talk a bit more about the importance of doing this in the **Be Interesting and Sociable** section later.

In the same way as you can try out different networking events, there's nothing necessarily wrong with experimenting and trying different channels/platforms on Social Media either. Even if they don't pan out to be ideal for you, at least you will be able to make some new contacts, develop some existing contacts perhaps and maybe increase your online presence as well. It's as equally important to know where you **don't** need to be as it is to know where you do!

And, of course, it might take some time to work this out so have patience (and purpose and keep practising).

Due to the nature of many platforms, it is possible (and in many cases easy) to provide links from the platforms on which you are not focussing to those on which your main activities are. There are also applications that can automate this. Using these approaches you can spread further across Social Media without dramatically increasing the amount of effort you need to put in.

How are you going to reuse your content?

A piece of content that you create for one Social Media platform has the potential to be reused on a different platform. For example, the transcript of a video on YouTube could be used as the basis for a blog post on your website, snippets from which could then be used as tweets on Twitter.

Repurposing content in this way can save you a lot of time on Social Media. To be able to do this effectively, though, you need to think it through in advance and work out what you are going to reuse, where and how. This advanced thinking needs to be part of your overall plan for your Social Media activities, which is something I'll come back to shortly.

Who is going to do it?

This might seem like a bit of an odd question to ask because you are most probably thinking that the obvious answer is you.

And in many cases that's what will happen. It will be you spending the time, creating the content and putting it wherever it needs to be put. In some regards, this is beneficial as you can directly manage your time and you are (probably) the world's best expert on you, what you do and how you do it. This makes you ideally placed to be able to do this.

But are you *really* the right person to do this?

Consider for a moment if you actually have the time to create your Social Media content, to keep on top of everything else that's going on out there that you want to keep track of and to reply to those things that you need to reply to.

You might be very good at what you do for a living but do you have the skills to create an interesting and dynamic online persona? The different platforms each have their idiosyncrasies and skillsets to use them effectively and let's not forget that a key element to your online presence is your website, the creation and maintenance of which requires a very different set of skills.

So it's important to consider who is actually going to be doing your Social Media activities and, if it's not you, who it's going to be and how much you are going to be getting them to be doing.

Only you can answer those questions and, of course, the answer might still be you!

But if it isn't, with regard to whoever will be doing it, for them to represent you as you would like to be represented, and to do this well, they will need to *properly* understand:

- you
- how you help people, i.e. what you do and how you do it
- your audience
- your aims

It's therefore important to spend time up front ensuring that they do understand all of that.

It is also possible to delegate representation at events and if you are doing this then the above still holds true in that whoever goes in your stead needs to properly understand what you do, how you do it and what their (i.e. your) goals are for attending that event. In my experience, however, this sort of delegated representation does not happen at events as much as it does on Social Media.

What is your plan?

OK – this section perhaps should have come first, as should your plan!

However, I've deliberately left it until last so I can refer back to what has been said previously.

Social Media is so easy to use – it's designed to be like that. And with things that are easy to use, they are easy to use badly and ineffectively, especially if not much thought goes into what is being done.

So whatever you do and wherever you do it, there needs to be method behind your activities. You need to have a plan to be able to do this effectively and this really comes back to what your aims are, what you want to achieve and with whom you want to do it.

As with any good plan:
- there are things that you will do right at the start of the execution of your plan, some of which might be "one-off" in nature, for example:
   - setting up your online persona in the first place
   - (more on that in a moment)
- there are things that you will do on a regular basis, for example:
   - replying to posts and connection requests
   - sending out content
   - repurposing content

- there are things that you will do on a more ad hoc basis, for example:
  - reacting to real-world events
  - specific "promotions" for you and your business

It's also important that your plan gets reviewed on a regular basis and gets revised accordingly as required.

So make sure you have a plan and don't "wade into" Social Media until you have!

Be Interesting and Sociable

For creating an online persona that is as interesting as you are in person.

Imagine going to an in-person networking event with a bit of a strange format. All that you are allowed to do is stand there, without talking, and hold up a piece of flipchart paper in front of you with things written on it that the others can see. Only the other people there can initiate the conversation with you but they don't have time to talk to everyone there. They have to choose who to talk to.

So what would make them choose to talk to *you*?

Whatever is on your flipchart paper!

What you put on your flipchart paper is hugely important in a situation like that and so you'd think very carefully about what you'd put on that sheet of paper or else they are going to find the others there more interesting than you and so talk to them and not you.

Now of course, in-person networking events don't work like that but, in essence, Social Media does. When someone is looking at information on Social Media, they are going to be drawn to the information that is more interesting to them and ignore the information that isn't. So whatever you put out there on Social Media is exactly akin to the flipchart paper from the previous analogy. If it is interesting to other people it will draw them to you. If it isn't, it won't and your activities will not be as effective as they could be.

What you are effectively aiming to do is to create an online persona that is as interesting to other people as you are in the real world. This online persona is the sum total of everything that you have put out there on Social Media. It might even include information that other people have said about you as well, which is something I'll come back to shortly.

In the same way as I encouraged you to think about how to **Be Interesting** at events, you need to do the same for Social Media too.

So, with regard to your online persona, let's consider:

- where you can put information
- how you can make it interesting
- how you can make it dynamic
- how you can make it more sociable
- how you can get others to add to it too
- how you can make it more like you

Where you can put information

You can normally attach some sort of description of yourself in each of the online platforms. How much space you have to do this varies from platform to platform so think of it as like being allowed different sizes of flipchart paper at the event I described earlier, so make use of them wisely.

Many platforms also provide the capability for you to add an image of yourself. In the same way you would consider what would be appropriate to wear if you were attending a networking event, do the same for your online image, i.e. consider carefully which picture to use to portray the appropriate image of yourself.

Also, if there is scope for a company-related image, it doesn't just have to be your company logo (although it's a good idea to potentially include that as well).

Use every opportunity (every piece of flipchart paper) you can for the platforms you use to present interesting information to those people that come along to find out about you.

And don't forget about your website! You have pretty much total control over what that looks like, what it says and how much you can say. Use this "virtual real estate" to your advantage. I've heard many digital marketeers say that the single purpose of Social Media is to steer people to your website, which is where you want them. When people are looking at your website they are almost a "captive" audience because they are focusing on you (and not the other hundreds of contacts they might have). So get them there and pique their interest in what you do...

How you can make your online persona interesting

In the **RAIL** Framework, I encouraged you to think about interesting information that you could share with others at your networking events. That information can be equally interesting on Social Media.

*In the section about the **RAIL** Framework, I referred to the Self-Questions Preparation Worksheet that I have created to help with preparation for a network event. Consideration of those questions, and the associated answers, will also help with determining what online content to create as part of your online persona. You can download that document from the Resources section on my website: www.intercog.co.uk.*

In the **ICE** Framework, I talked about how you can creatively answer the question "What do you do?". A simple approach to that was to talk about how you help people, about what you do that makes a positive difference to those other people, about the "pain points" of theirs that you can address, reduce and even remove.

This approach works equally well on Social Media too. By looking at things from your audience's perspective and positioning your content in that way, you will come across in a more relatable way and that will be better received by your audience. So make it about them, not about you.

If the platform has the scope for a large amount of information, put the best bits at the top so they get read first. Don't make your audience wade through lots of text before they get to those interesting bits, because they won't!

(This is where I say, "And don't forget about your website!" again).

Some platforms, however, only show "snippets" of your information and then provide the ability for people to "see more...". On platforms like these it is even more important to have that "attention grabbing" information first so that they are enticed to then see more of your information. Using the analogy from earlier, you only have a small piece of flipchart paper in those circumstances, so you need to make the most of it.

So far, I have been implicitly talking about people just reading about you. However, if you were to ask someone if they found it more interesting to read about you or to actually talk to you then, in the vast majority of cases, they would say to talk to you. Of course they would, it's a more interactive, dynamic and effective way to communicate.

At a networking event, it's not really an issue because that's what naturally happens – people talk to each other. However, on Social Media it isn't what naturally happens. What naturally happens is normally text and images, or in other words, lots of reading.

The next thing to therefore consider here is adding video to your online persona. The use of video content has become more and more popular over recent years and can potentially portray you in a more interesting way than simple text or images can. It's also rapidly becoming the "de facto" way of consuming online content and so not only is it a more interesting way of coming across, it's also becoming the preferred/expected way for users to do it.

Video content can be delivered in a pre-recorded format that can be posted and then viewed at a time of choice for the audience. It is possible for viewer interaction however, through mechanics such as leaving comments, comments to which you can then reply.

Video content can also be presented as a live experience and this is much more akin to speaking to somebody at an actual networking event. Webinars, online meetings and live streaming technologies can all facilitate this. Due to its "live" nature, this format also provides the opportunity for instant interaction with your audience. The live content can also be recorded and posted later to get the best of both video worlds, so to speak.

Regardless of whether your video is pre-recorded or live, it has become easier and easier to create and share that content and some platforms have evolved purely for that media type. That being said, just because something is *technically* easy to do, it does not mean that it is easy to do well or that people are comfortable doing it either. Like most things, creating effective video content requires knowledge, skills and confidence in order to do it well but done well, it can really increase the interest level that people have in you.

If only somebody had written a book on "How to be BETTER at PRESENTING" that included the knowledge and skills that would give people confidence and help them to create effective video content for their online persona and to deliver live streams well...

And as the final thing to say about having an interesting online persona, I'd like to adapt Dale Carnegie's quote again. The original quote:

"People are interested in people who are interested in them"

becomes

"People are interested in people who are interested in them and are therefore interested in people who are also interested in other people".

So how does this link to your online persona and making it more interesting? Well, by providing recommendations/reviews/feedback for other people, or "liking" or "sharing" their content, this implies that you are therefore interested in those people. By being interested in those people, other people who, for example, are connected to those people will become interested in you because of the interest you have shown. By definition, therefore you become more interesting (to them).

Providing recommendations/reviews/feedback for other people, or "liking" or "sharing" their content also has the side effect of increasing your own online presence as well as people would see your activity when looking at someone else's information. That will in turn make your online persona appear to be more dynamic, which leads me nicely into...

How you can make your online persona dynamic

In the vast majority of cases, something that changes is going to be more interesting than something that doesn't. Therefore, another way of making your online persona more interesting is to make it change more or, in other words, to make it more dynamic.

There are three aspects to how dynamic your online persona is:

- how active you are
- how reactive you are
- how proactive you are

How active you are is very much down to how much you are "doing" on Social Media and that of course is driven by the level to which you would like or need to go (B, C, or D). At level B you have a passive presence, i.e. people can find out information about you but you don't really interact with them. In this case it would be fair to say that you are not very active, your online persona is not very dynamic. At levels C and D you are choosing to do more and so are clearly therefore more active (and therefore more dynamic).

How active you are is effectively driven by how much you interact with other people and therefore it's really all about how reactive and/or proactive you are.

Things to which you can react include:
- connection requests
- invitations
- posts, content etc that other people create which may, or may not, reference you directly
- real world events

And ways in which you can be proactive include:
- updating your information regularly
- making connection requests
- sending invitations
- generating content (posts, videos etc)
- following up with connections on a regular basis

*Back in the **RAIL** Framework, when I was talking about what to do after an event, I suggested that you might continue to stay in touch with your contacts by sending them "useful stuff". The same premise holds for contacts you have met through Social Media in that it's a great way to maintain those relationships. In fact, it's possible that Social Media would be the way that you would send things to your "event-originated" contacts as well!*

So how active your online persona is really is just a combination of how reactive and proactive you are. And the more active you are, the more dynamic you'll be. And the more dynamic you are, the more interesting you will appear to everyone else.

How you can make your online persona more sociable

It's not called *Social* Media by accident!

Many of the platforms therefore provide the capability to build social elements into what you do. Likes, smileys and emojis to name but a few.

A lot of other elements, however, require that you put the social part in yourself – so do so!

Take connection requests, for example. Most platforms make it easy to send such a request and often offer "templates" for those requests. However, although it might be easy to use the offered suggestion, don't. Using these templates is a very impersonal way to do it. There's no "you" in that request and, perhaps more importantly, there's no "them" either.

So avoid just pinging out generic, potentially system-generated requests. Tailor the request to that individual including, for example, why it is that you are making this request, what has led you to do so etc. It's exactly the same premise as tailoring what you do at events when you approach someone there.

Some platforms allow you to see who has viewed your information. The fact that someone has done this provides you with an easy way to personalise a connection request/message: "Hi. I noticed that you had viewed my profile and so I was curious what led you to find me and how I might therefore be able to help you." Again, how you help people is part of your positioning.

And the same applies to accepting connection requests. Don't just hit the "Accept" button. Take the time to add a bit of "you" into your reply. It's also important to tailor your reply to the requestor and to relate to them and their request in your reply. Thanking them for their request, and implicitly therefore their interest in you, is also a good thing to do.

Remember these requests or acceptances are only the first step in the relationship-building process. Don't be tempted to bombard them with too much information in this point – there's time for that as the relationship develops. In the same way that you wouldn't walk up to someone at a networking event and then just talk at them for a few minutes without letting them get a word in themselves, don't do the online equivalent either!

The above two points relate back to earlier in the book when I talked about the **PROWESS** Framework which was all about how to exude confidence whilst networking at events. Two of the letters in that framework relate to this aspect of being sociable:

- Be **Outgoing**
- Be **Welcoming**

Being **outgoing** was about having the courage at events to approach people and start a conversation. The Social Media equivalent to this is sending that connection request and for some people, this is equally as scary as doing it in-person. It is, however, technically much simpler to do – you just have to click/tap and it's done! There's no concept of open or closed groups to deal with and there's no physical distance over which you have to travel that often puts people off doing so.

But it still takes courage to click on the button, to be outgoing.

What can make it less scary, though, is to have thought ahead about who to approach and how to approach them, i.e. what to say as part of your connection request. This planning ahead, as mentioned above, gives confidence via Social Media in the same way as it does at a networking event.

Thinking now about being **welcoming**, I talked about this earlier in relation to when people approached and joined your group at an event. The Social Media equivalent is receiving a connection request. Again, it's an easy thing to do to just click/tap the "Accept" button but it's not a very welcoming response. So, as described above, take a moment as part of accepting the request to personalise your reply, to be more welcoming.

This also applies to your website. If you make it really easy for people to get in contact with you, potentially also with appropriate wording to actively encourage them to do so, then you will appear more welcoming to them. Simple links to click on, or contact forms to easily complete, facilitate those connection steps. And make sure that you then respond to them *personally*, even if you have got some sort of automated "Thank You" response. It all adds to that feeling of being welcomed.

How you can get others to add to your online persona

There's nothing quite like someone saying something nice about you to really make you look good in somebody else's eyes. This is as equally true via Social Media as it is in person. In some ways, however it's even better if done on Social Media.

Consider, for a moment, a kind comment that someone makes about you at a networking event. It's great and can have a hugely beneficial impact for you with those who hear it. However, over time the particulars fade from the recipient's memory and so potentially does its impact. That comment is also only heard by those there at the time, although there is the potential for it to be passed on (with all of the normal Chinese Whispers that go along with that of course!).

Consider now, for example, a recommendation someone does for you on LinkedIn. It's clear in its meaning and its impact at the time it's created and for ever more (practically). Everyone who comes to your LinkedIn page will see it. It's a lot more permanent and pervasive than a comment at a networking event. It's especially powerful if the person reading it knows the person who has given it, in the same way as it would if it had been made at an actual event.

When you consider the different platforms that you use for Social Media, there are many and different ways that other people can therefore add to your online persona by talking about you, by mentioning what you have done for them, how you have done it and what difference it has made. As with in-person events, many of these mentions come in an unsolicited way but some of them don't, some of them you can ask for. It is a fairly common practice for people to ask other people to create Social Media content for recommendations, reviews and positive feedback for work done. The request has to be made in the correct way, of course, but it can be made, and people are normally happy to do it as well.

The event equivalent is to ask someone to "put in a good word for you" and whilst that isn't unheard of, it's requested so much less in this context than in Social Media.

Also, many platforms have the functionality for people to "like" or "share" content that other people have created. If people do this for your content then it will increase the scope and interest level of your online persona as well. In fact, it pays to **Be Welcoming** again in that you can make it clear that you actively welcome other people sharing your content. Let them know that you are happy for them to:

- "like" your content
- "share" your content
- comment on your content
- link to your website, posts etc
- pass on "stuff" that you have sent them
- etc

How you can make your online persona more like you

Social Media presents you with so many opportunities to interject a bit of *you* in what you do and you need to make the most of those opportunities because, ultimately, "people buy from people".

This phrase has been used for many years to neatly allude to one of the underlying principles of networking that people's buying decisions are fundamentally based on who they are buying from, how well they know and trust them and, in many cases, how much they like them. It's the familiar "know, like, trust" trilogy which, when you stop and think about it, is really all about relationships.

And for those relationships to develop, people need to get to know *you*. In many ways this happens naturally at events as you talk to people over time. Exactly the same mindset is also therefore needed on Social Media, so make sure that, in everything that you do, you take a personal and sociable approach. It might be tempting to take the easier (and potentially quicker) automated/suggested option, but don't.

*This relates back to the "**Don't Sell, Build!**" core principle in that, although I might be using the terms "buy" and "sell" here, it essentially comes back to relationships that you have with the other contacts in your network and the quality of those relationships. Putting it another way, it's all about the size of the dots in your network and bigger is indeed better!*

Further Information

The *"Interact better. Achieve more."* Series

This is the second title in the "***Interact** better. **Achieve** more.*" series. The other titles in the series are:

- *How to be BETTER at* PRESENTING - In Person and Online
- *How to be BETTER at* COMMUNICATING - In Person and Online

How to be BETTER at PRESENTING - In Person and Online

Do any of these scenarios sound familiar:

- The thought of doing a presentation keeps you awake at night and you'd almost rather do anything else than that looming presentation. If only presentations didn't make you feel so bad, maybe you might even look forward to doing them one day.
- You know you've got to deliver some presentations and that it's important to come across positively whilst doing them. You've not done many before, though, so it would be nice to know how to do them well.
- You're great at what you do but when it comes to telling other people about it you're rubbish! You'd really like to tell them what you do in a way that they would understand and remember.
- You do a lot of presenting and you're good at it. You know that you could be even better, you want to be even better, but don't know how to take things to the next level.
- Your company is great, your team is great and you get asked to tender for lots of opportunities, which is also great! But you don't win as many of them as you would like to. You're thinking, "What is it about our presenting style that's getting in the way of our own success?".

These are all examples of where people are not achieving what they would like to when they are presenting. There are many more examples like these and maybe you have your own variation on the above as well.

In all of these cases, though, what's stopping people achieving what they want is actually very easy to identify – they don't know **how** to be a better presenter.

So this book will give you that knowledge, the knowledge of how to be a better presenter, together with the associated skills to do it.

When you put that knowledge and those skills into practice, not only will you become a better presenter, you will also become a more confident presenter as well.

And by being a better presenter with greater confidence, you will achieve whatever it is that you want to achieve.

With the ever-increasing use of technology in business, this book also includes considerations for presenting online/remotely.

How to be BETTER at COMMUNICATING - In Person and Online

Do any of these scenarios sound familiar:

- You thought you had said one thing and they thought you'd said something else (and vice versa). It didn't end well...
- Other people just don't seem to get what you're saying, even though it's perfectly clear in your own head. If only they could understand what you mean.
- You don't understand the points that others are trying to make. Life would be so much easier if you did.
- Meetings, meetings, meetings! You spend way too much time in meetings. If only they were better planned and more effective.
- Giving somebody feedback always feels a bit awkward. It would be great to know how to do it so that it was comfortably given, well received and properly appreciated.
- Interviews are unnecessarily stressful and unsuccessful, either for the interviewee, the interviewer or both. Surely there must be an easier and better way?

Being able to communicate effectively is a core skill and is vital for achieving what you would like to achieve. Unfortunately, it's not always as straightforward as it might appear and less than effective communication can lead to a wide variety of undesirable results (like those above).

The foundation of being able to communicate effectively is a core knowledge set that is applicable to all occasions when communication is needed. On top of this foundation is specific knowledge that is required for particular occasions, e.g. for running meetings, giving feedback or being interviewed etc.

This book provides a set of frameworks for both the foundation and specific knowledge that is required to communicate effectively. In essence, it will give you the knowledge and skills for being a better communicator.

When you put that knowledge and those skills into practice, not only will you become a better communicator, you will also become more confident as a result.

By being a better communicator with greater confidence, you will therefore achieve whatever it is that you want to achieve.

As with all of the titles in this series, with the ever-increasing use of technology in business, this book also includes considerations for communicating online/remotely.

About the Author

Mike moved back to his native Staffordshire in 2009 and set up his training and coaching business Intercog. At that time, Mike's business network had exactly two people in it!

Since then, Mike has built up his network to include hundreds of local connections and the majority of the work that he has done over that time has come via the connections in his network and referrals that have been made to him through his network.

Over those years, Mike has also helped hundreds of other people to connect and to build their own networks. Mike has done this through the design and facilitation of entertaining and interactive networking events which he delivers for a number of local businesses and organisations, including a number of Chambers of Commerce.

Mike also helps people to become more effective, more confident networkers through the combination of knowledge transfers, training sessions and one-to-one coaching.

His goal with all of these activities is to help people to interact better and achieve more of what they want to.

Mike can be contacted via his website at www.intercog.co.uk.